Barbados

DIRECTIONS

WRITTEN AND RESEARCHED BY

Adam Vaitilingam

THIS EDITION UPDATED AND RESEARCHED BY

Ross Velton

ROUGH
GUIDES

NEW YORK • LONDON • DELHI
www.roughguides.com

Contents

Introduction to

Barbados

Pulling in Caribbean first-timers and experienced travellers in equal measure, Barbados is justifiably one of the most popular islands in the region. Certain pleasures are quite obvious – the delightful climate, the gorgeous blue sea and brilliant white-sand beaches – but an engaging blend of cultures and a relatively balanced approach to development help set it apart from similar sun-drenched destinations.

For more than three centuries Barbados was a British colony and, perhaps unsurprisingly, it retains something of a British feel: the place names; the cricket, horse-racing and polo; the Anglican parish churches; even a hilly district known as Scotland. But the Britishness can be exaggerated, for this is a distinctly West Indian country, covered by a patchwork of sugar cane fields and dotted with tiny rum shops. Calypso is the music of choice, flying fish the favoured food and contemporary cultural influences are as likely to emanate from America as from Europe. Meanwhile, the people of Barbados, known as Barbadians, or Bajans colloquially, are as warm and welcoming as you'll find anywhere.

Among the island's more traditional attractions are its evocative plantation houses, colourful botanical gardens and proud military

When to visit

For many visitors Barbados's tropical **climate** – hot and sunny year-round – is its leading attraction. The weather is at its best during the high season (mid-December to mid-April), with rainfall low and the heat tempered by cooling trade winds. Things get noticeably hotter during the summer and, particularly in September and October, the humidity can become oppressive. September is also the most threatening month of the annual hurricane season, which runs from June through October, though it's worth bearing in mind that, on average, the big blows only hit about once a decade.

▲ Paradise Beach

forts and signal stations. The capital, Bridgetown, is a lively place, with an excellent national museum, some good nightlife and numerous duty-free shopping opportunities. Then there are the beaches, from the often-crowded strips such as Accra Beach and Mullins Bay to tiny but superb patches of palm-fringed sand like Bottom Bay in the southeast. And all around the island you can find first-rate food and drink; particularly delightful are the many bars and restaurants that overlook the ocean.

▼ St James Parish

INTRODUCTION

Despite the hordes of visitors who descend on the island, development has been more discreet than you might expect, with many of the facilities owned by Bajans, a distinct lack of private beaches and (KFC excepted) relatively few signs of the fast-food franchises that blight other islands in the region. Admittedly, there are areas on both the south and west coasts where tourism is utterly dominant and Bajans massively outnumbered by European and American visitors, but they're easy to get away from, if you want. Jump on a bus or rent a car to see the rest of the island: the sugar-growing central parishes, the thinly populated and little-explored north, and the ruggedly beautiful east coast, where you can hike for miles along the beach with only sea birds and the occasional surfer in sight.

Barbados
AT A GLANCE

AROUND BRIDGETOWN

The outskirts of Bridgetown hold some colonial and modern treasures, from the restored military buildings that surround the Garrison Savannah – now the island's main racetrack – to the rum factories that continue to churn out top-quality liquor.

Garrison Savannah

BRIDGETOWN

Easily the busiest and most populated place on the island, Bridgetown is the nation's capital. Lively, colourful and buzzing with the activities of city life, the place is mostly modern and functional, and remains home to the country's main businesses, schools, churches, shops and markets.

Bridgetown

THE SOUTH COAST

Stretching east of Bridgetown towards the airport, the south coast is the island's main resort area. Swarming with people but rarely feeling crowded, there are plenty of fantastic white-sand beaches and enough hotels and restaurants to house and feed a small army.

▲ Worthing Beach, the south coast

THE SOUTHEAST COAST

East of the airport the roads wind through fields of sugar cane and small villages characterized by colourful chattel houses and tiny rum shops. Once the haunt of smugglers and wreckers, the beaches of this little-developed area – from idyllic Bottom Bay to wilder Harrismith Beach – are some of the finest on the island.

THE WEST COAST

A sparkling strip of sand runs for many miles north of Bridgetown and, though dotted with the homes of the rich and famous, remains open to all. A couple of small towns stud the coast: resort-like Holetown, with its wide selection of restaurants, shops and banks, and the quiet, charming and largely untouristed Speightstown, once a thriving and wealthy port.

CENTRAL BARBADOS

Acre after acre of sugar cane fields cover the central part of Barbados, interspersed with small areas of ancient forest and the odd historical or natural

attraction – welcome diversions from the beach.

THE NORTH

Many visitors make a quick tour through the north to see green monkeys at the island's wildlife reserve and some ruggedly set beaches, where the Atlantic lashes against the precipitous cliffs and the surf flies across the breeze.

THE EAST COAST

This quiet part of the island, with its miles of empty beaches and crashing waves, small but picturesque villages and spectacular cliff-top scenery, is prime territory for surfers, hikers and others wanting to escape the masses.

▶ Cove Bay, the north

Ideas

The big six

There are a handful of attractions that, taken together, will give you a fully rounded picture of what makes Barbados such a special place. Seeing all six of the sights listed here will take you to nearly every corner of the island, from the colonial architecture outside Bridgetown to the windswept cliffs along the Atlantic coast, and even down into its subterranean depths.

▲ West coast sunsets

Always spectacular, whether you get to see the legendary "green flash" or not.

P.86 ▸ THE WEST COAST

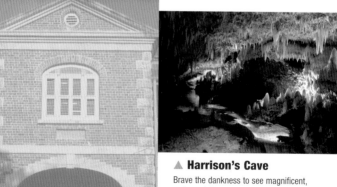

▲ Harrison's Cave

Brave the dankness to see magnificent, eerie rock formations and limpid pools of icy water.

P.104 ▸ CENTRAL BARBADOS

▲ Barbados Museum

Simply unmissable, with superb exhibits on key aspects of the country's past and present.

P.62 ▸ AROUND BRIDGETOWN

▲ Garrison Savannah

Fabulous Georgian buildings surround the old military parade ground, now home to the island's main racetrack.

P.61 ▸ AROUND BRIDGETOWN

▲ The view from Hackleton's Cliff

Sensational views over the east coast make this a worthy detour as you travel around the island.

P.118 ▸ THE EAST COAST

◀ Speightstown

The island's charmingly dilapidated second town makes a defiant stand against the tourist development along the west coast.

P.93 ▸ THE WEST COAST

Swimming spots

Most visitors to Barbados head straight for the beach for a plunge in the gorgeous turquoise sea, with the most popular beaches getting especially packed at weekends and in high season. While the west coast normally sees calmer seas, the frequent swells on the south coast – particularly in the southeast – make for great body-surfing or just splashing around.

▲ Mullins Bay

Famous for its crowded beach bar, this splendid strip is located up in the northwest near Speightstown.

P.92 ▶ THE WEST COAST

▲ Miami Beach

Head to this protected little bay to lounge in the sea or chill with a book under the casuarina trees.

P.73 ▶ THE SOUTH COAST

▶ Accra Beach

Renowned beach with a lively vibe – a great place to make new friends.

▶ Paynes Bay Beach

A laid-back, family atmosphere, plenty of facilities and sea turtles to swim with have made this one of the west coast's most popular beaches.

▲ Dover Beach

This long stretch of powdery sand on the south coast is good for light body-surfing almost year-round.

▼ Crane Beach

A little remote, but a clear contender for one of the best Caribbean beaches.

Colonial Barbados

Barbados has a rich colonial heritage. The British, who ruled the country for over three centuries, left behind a fascinating architectural trove, including many churches, military forts and signal stations and grand plantation houses. But the colonial legacy is not limited to fine British buildings: the brightly coloured chattel houses, in particular, are an enduring testimony to the ingenuity of the Barbadian people.

▼ Chattel houses

The portable home – just a great invention.

P.72 ▶ THE SOUTH COAST

▼ Gun Hill Signal Station

The most impressive of the military communication centres that were built after the island's only major slave uprising.

P.103 ▶ CENTRAL BARBADOS

▲ St Nicholas Abbey

The oldest residence on the island, dating back to the earliest days of colonial settlement.

P.112 ▸ THE NORTH

▲ Tyrol Cot

This magnificent house was formerly home to two of the country's prime ministers.

P.65 ▸ AROUND BRIDGETOWN

▶ Codrington College

Venerable theological college, founded with the fortunes made from the sugar plantations that once stood here.

P.115 ▸ THE EAST COAST

▲ Harford Chambers

Every country has its much-loved lawyers; here they're housed in seventeenth-century splendour.

P.54 ▸ BRIDGETOWN

Outdoor activities

Dragging yourself away from the sand and sea won't be easy during a stay in Barbados, but there are plenty of other outdoor activities waiting if you do. More and more of the old sugar cane fields are being given over to new pursuits, from golf to clay pigeon shooting, while the island's natural splendour offers good opportunities for hiking and horse-riding trips.

▲ Tandem parasailing

There's no better way for honeymooning couples to bond than by floating together above the clear blue waters of the Caribbean.

P.140 ▸ ESSENTIALS

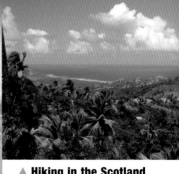

▲ Hiking in the Scotland District

Take to the hills on foot in this ruggedly beautiful area, and leave the masses behind.

P.118 ▸ THE EAST COAST

▲ Road tennis

Bizarre but utterly addictive game, played on flat roads throughout Barbados.

P.106 ▸ CENTRAL BARBADOS

▼ Horse-riding on the beach

Hold on as your faithful steed takes you through picturesque countryside and down to the beach.

P.140 ▸ ESSENTIALS

▲ Bird-watching at Graeme Hall Nature Sanctuary

The island's best birding is around a peaceful swamp not far from the tourist hordes.

P.69 ▸ THE SOUTH COAST

▼ Barbados Golf Club

Unlike other courses on the island, a completely unpretentious place open to all.

P.140 ▸ ESSENTIALS

Gourmet restaurants

Barbados has some of the finest restaurants in the Caribbean, which showcase great chefs and cuisines from around the world and superb local ingredients, particularly those freshly pulled from the ocean. Most of the classy places are along the west coast – often with spectacular locations overlooking the sea – and new spots pop up every season.

▲ Josef's

One of the finest restaurants on the south coast, with a superb location by the sea.

P.77 ▸ THE SOUTH COAST

▼ Zen

Splash out on classic Japanese and Thai cuisine and relish the immaculate vantage point high above Crane Beach.

P.85 ▸ THE SOUTHEAST COAST

▶ Mango's by the Sea

Not as famous as some of its west coast peers, but the meat and seafood here are just sensational.

P.99 ▶ THE WEST COAST

▼ The Tides

A romantic oceanfront setting complimented perfectly by some of the island's best cooking.

P.100 ▶ THE WEST COAST

▶ The Cliff

Enjoy excellent international food in a magnificent cliff-top location.

P.98 ▶ THE WEST COAST

▼ Daphne's

Superb Italian–Caribbean fusion cuisine has established this as a west coast favourite.

P.98 ▶ THE WEST COAST

Green Barbados

Although the virgin forest that once blanketed Barbados was largely cleared decades ago to allow planters to grow sugar cane, small tracts do remain, permitting visitors a glimpse of the island's original state. Elsewhere, you'll find vibrant, flower-filled botanical gardens created with enormous care and attention; seldom crowded with human visitors, they are often teeming with colourful birdlife.

▲ Welchman Hall Gully

Wander through this fissure in the rock and see the island's lush vegetation as the first visitors must have done.

P.104 ▸ CENTRAL BARBADOS

▼ Andromeda Botanical Gardens

Beautifully landscaped gardens of local and imported flora, with stunning ocean views to boot.

P.120 ▸ THE EAST COAST

▲ The Flower Forest

A converted sugar plantation, now sprawling with flowers, shrubs and a variety of palms.

P.106 ▸ CENTRAL BARBADOS

▶ Turner's Hall Woods

Ancient silk-cotton trees and unique jack-in-the-box trees are the highlights in this small piece of original forest.

P.106 ▸ CENTRAL BARBADOS

▼ Orchid World

Get lost in the profusion of colour provided by thousands of these exotic blooms.

P.104 ▸ CENTRAL BARBADOS

Churches and synagogues

The influence of the first European settlers is evident in Barbados's many churches, with the main parish churches – as well as the synagogue in Bridgetown – dating from the early colonial days of the mid-seventeenth century. Between the elegant cathedral in Bridgetown and the smaller churches scattered across the island, you'll find something to tweak your interest, whether it's hand-carved detail, atmospheric cemeteries or lovely cliff-top views.

▲ St Peter's Parish Church

Rebuilt after a hurricane and impeccably restored after a fire, St Peter's is one of the main landmarks in Speightstown.

P.93 ▸ THE WEST COAST

▲ Christ Church Parish Church

The stories of ghoulish happenings in the Chase family vault here lend this place a slightly haunted air.

P.72 ▸ THE SOUTH COAST

▼ St Michael's Cathedral

One of Bridgetown's most impressive sights, this is the island's main place of worship.

P.56 ▸ BRIDGETOWN

▲ The synagogue

Located in Bridgetown's oldest section, the Jewish synagogue preserves a slice of the island's early history.

P.55 ▸ BRIDGETOWN

▶ St John's Parish Church

The graveyard here is believed to be the burial site of the final surviving descendant of Emperor Constantine XI.

P.118 ▸ THE EAST COAST

▼ St James Parish Church

Barbados's prettiest church stands a stone's throw from the beach.

P.91 ▸ THE WEST COAST

Rum and sugar

The old English expression "as wealthy as a planter" certainly held true for the grand estates of Barbados, which brought huge riches to its sugar barons as well as great misery to the thousands of slaves and indentured labourers who toiled in the fields and in the boiling-houses. Although sugar has declined in importance to Barbados's economy, it remains an integral part of the country's history: the island's main festival of Crop Over still celebrates the end of the harvest, while rum – a by-product of sugar – remains a vital export.

▼ Malibu Beach Club & Visitor Centre

The company's renowned coconut-flavoured rum is made here; when you've seen (and tasted) enough, the beach is great, too.

P.65 › AROUND BRIDGETOWN

▼ Morgan Lewis Sugar Mill

The only working sugar mill on the island, tucked away in the quiet northeast.

P.111 › THE NORTH

▲ The Foursquare Rum Factory and Heritage Park

Modern factory with all the latest equipment and even its own little art gallery.

P.83 ▸ THE SOUTHEAST COAST

▼ Mount Gay Rum Factory

The aroma of rum coming from this factory will have you reeling, even before you've gone anywhere near the free snifter.

P.64 ▸ AROUND BRIDGETOWN

▼ Sir Frank Hutson Sugar Museum and Portvale Sugar Factory

A worthy testament to the island's pre-tourism source of income.

P.92 ▸ THE WEST COAST

Bars and lounges

You'll find plenty of places to drink in Barbados, in the company of both locals and your fellow visitors. One of the island's most enjoyable features is its diverse collection of tiny rum shops, dotted across the island, where the day's big issues are debated over a cold Banks beer or a half bottle of rum and a game of dominoes. On the coast, almost everywhere has food as its primary focus – although many of these places double as lively drinking spots.

▲ Carib Beach Bar

Come here on a Sunday evening for a major beachside "lime".

P.78 ▸ THE SOUTH COAST

▲ Nelson's Arms

Horatio Nelson is still a hero at this longstanding pub, even if they're not sure what to do with his statue in town.

P.59 ▸ BRIDGETOWN

▶ Bubba's Sports Bar

The place to go for those serious about cheering on their favourite team.

P.78 ▶ THE SOUTH COAST

▲ Upstairs at Olive's

Mellow, comfortable bar in the heart of Holetown – the perfect place to end an evening.

P.100 ▶ THE WEST COAST

▼ Rum shops

Polish up your knowledge of cricket and dominoes for a session with the locals.

P.134 ▶ ESSENTIALS

▼ Pravda

Sip cocktails with beautiful people at this recent addition to the Barbados bar scene.

P.79 ▶ THE SOUTH COAST

Hidden beaches

You rarely have to stray far to find a quiet beach in Barbados. Some of the best are tucked away in the less touristed southeast: typically small, secluded and studded with swaying palm trees, you'll get them to yourself for the day if you're lucky. On the east coast, the surf and tides can make swimming dangerous, but the beaches are often deserted and ideal for a solitary stroll.

▼ Cove Bay

Gorgeous spot with endless views along the entire length of the east coast.

P.113 ▶ THE NORTH

▼ Bottom Bay

This stunning white-sand beach is a photographer's dream.

P.83 ▶ THE SOUTHEAST COAST

◀ Long Beach

Not the prettiest of Barbados's beaches, but definitely the best place to hunt for driftwood.

▼ Bathsheba

A long brown swathe of deserted beach cherished by sea birds and surfers.

▲ Harrismith Beach

This wild but picturesque place is ideal for setting up a picnic for two away from the crowds.

▼ Martin's Bay

Completely off the tourist track, this peaceful bay often sees the local fishing fleet pulled up on the sands.

Indulgent Barbados

Barbados is one of the more exclusive islands in the Caribbean, and there are a number of decadent ways to blow a fortune. With the island pulling in its share of the mega-rich, five-star hotels, sumptuous villas and top-class restaurants abound; and the influence of the British upper class is all too apparent in the country's predilection for activities such as horse-racing and polo.

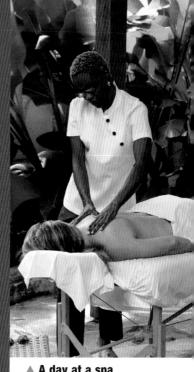

▲ A day at a spa

If the beach just isn't doing it for you, find complete relaxation at the Suga Suga Spa.

P.93 ▶ THE WEST COAST

▲ Attending a polo match

Don't worry if you don't know the rules – you'll feel like royalty watching this aristocratic sport.

P.88 ▶ THE WEST COAST

▶ Brunch at La Mer

Hungover or not, the magnificent Sunday brunch here will get you back on your feet.

P.99 ▶ THE WEST COAST

▼ A night at Lone Star hotel

With the waves crashing a few feet from your veranda, you can't beat this for romance.

P.97 ▶ THE WEST COAST

▼ Cocktails at Sandy Lane

Hob-nob with the rich and famous at the legendary and spectacularly revamped west coast hotel.

P.89 ▶ THE WEST COAST

▼ Renting a villa

You can spend literally thousands of dollars per night on your dream home-away-from-home.

P.132 ▶ ESSENTIALS

Crafts and souvenirs

The island isn't famed for its crafts, but visitors will find an abundance of eye-catching items to take home as mementos of their stay. The main streets of Bridgetown regularly draw flocks of cruise ship passengers in search of gifts and bargains, while elsewhere on the island particularly good souvenir-hunting options can be found around Holetown on the west coast.

▲ Duty-free shops on Broad Street

Compete with the cruise ship hordes in spending on low-cost liquor, jewellery and a lot more.

P.57 ▸ BRIDGETOWN

▲ Shell Gallery

Beautiful collection of shells, sold individually or in cleverly crafted works of art.

P.95 ▸ THE WEST COAST

▲ Earthworks Pottery

Browse pieces from the pottery's factory, as well as handcrafted items made by the potters up on nearby Chalky Mount.

P.88 ▸ THE WEST COAST

▶ Chattel House Village

Sniff out gifts for the folks back home at this pretty little chattel house estate.

P.90 ▸ THE WEST COAST

▼ Pelican Craft Centre

The best range of souvenirs on the island is found in this attractive complex on the western edge of Bridgetown.

P.58 ▸ BRIDGETOWN

Barbados after dark

Barbados may not be a major player in the Caribbean music scene, but its handful of pubs and clubs make up in enthusiasm and buzz what they may lack in cutting-edge music. You'll find most of the action on the south coast, particularly around St Lawrence Gap, where venues lay on great sounds after the sun goes down, while for many visitors an evening's clubbing in Bridgetown's The *Boatyard* or *Harbour Lights* ranks among the highlights of their trip.

▼ Club Xtreme

A seductive mix of dazzling lights, pumping sounds and dirty moves makes this the island's premier dance club.

P.79 ▶ THE SOUTH COAST

▼ Bajan Roots and Rhythms

A lavish evening of traditional Barbadian music and dance complements a tasty supper.

P.79 ▶ THE SOUTH COAST

▲ The Boatyard

This great beachfront club is always busy, especially on the all-you-can-drink party nights.

P.60 ▸ BRIDGETOWN

▼ McBride's Pub

Irish pub that pulls in a good crowd every night, especially on Wednesdays for the live reggae.

P.79 ▸ THE SOUTH COAST

▲ Harbour Lights

A smaller alternative to *The Boatyard*, where you'll get just as drunk – only here they'll drive you back to your hotel at night's end.

P.60 ▸ BRIDGETOWN

▼ The Ship Inn

This large pub-cum-nightclub is good for a boogie, a flirt or just a quiet(ish) pint.

P.79 ▸ THE SOUTH COAST

Water sports

The confirmed beach addict and the water sports fanatic will be equally at home in Barbados, where the beaches are appealingly varied and numerous operators offer a wide range of ocean-based activities. You could easily spend a week exploring all the options, which, thanks to the competition, are generally reasonably priced. For diving and snorkelling trips, in particular, operators will often arrange to come and collect you from your hotel.

▲ Diving

Whether you're diving on a shipwreck or a reef, Barbados's fish and coral will have you reeling in awe.

P.137 ▸ ESSENTIALS

▼ Snorkelling

Look out for turtles on the west coast, or head out on a boat trip for some great coral heads.

P.138 ▸ ESSENTIALS

▶ Kayaking

If paddling about in the sea is more your speed, check out the kayak rental at Charles Watersports in Dover.

P.139 ▸ ESSENTIALS

▼ Windsurfing at Silver Sands

The fair winds that blow here draw windsurfers from all over the world.

P.73 ▸ THE SOUTH COAST

▲ Surfing in the soup bowl

Consistently good waves make the quiet east coast resort of Bathsheba a paradise for surfers.

P.120 ▸ THE EAST COAST

Bajan specialities

Whatever you do in Barbados, be sure to try some of the island's speciality food and drink. Local breweries and distilleries churn out top-notch beers and rums, while an innovative local culinary tradition means that you can sample some superb dishes that you've never seen before.

▲ **Banks beer**

Known as the Beer of Barbados, and available everywhere.

P.134 ▸ ESSENTIALS

▼ Breadfruit

An island staple for centuries, courtesy of Captain Bligh of the *Bounty*.

P.134 ▸ ESSENTIALS

▼ Pudding and souse

Don't ask what it is – just sit back and enjoy one of the finest of the local offerings.

P.134 ▸ ESSENTIALS

▲ Cou-cou

OK – corn meal and okra may not sound like haute cuisine, but this is quite superb. *The Waterfront Café* is one of the many places that serve it.

P.60 ▸ BRIDGETOWN

▼ A bottle of Mount Gay extra old rum

Let everyone else drink the basic white stuff in their cocktails; this is for the true aficionado.

P.64 ▸ AROUND BRIDGETOWN

Barbados calendar

Bajans will use any excuse to put on a party, and there is no shortage of opportunities during the year. Traditional festivals celebrate matters as diverse as the local fishing fleet or the end of the sugar harvest; more modern additions to the calendar include a great festival of classical music at Holders House. International cricket matches remain one of the highlights of the year for many Bajans – despite the West Indies' slip in the world rankings – and the island slows down dramatically when there's a game on.

▼ Oistins Fish Festival

You've eaten plenty at the town's famous market – now celebrate Oistins' fishing industry at the country's quirkiest festival.

P.135 › ESSENTIALS

▼ Holetown Festival

Lively parades, street performers and stalls mark this week-long festival celebrated each February.

P.135 › ESSENTIALS

▲ Crop Over

Simply the best of the Barbadian festivals, and among the finest carnivals in the Caribbean.

P.136 › ESSENTIALS

▲ Test cricket

Always a major crowd-puller, with matches played at the impressively revamped Kensington Oval.

P.64 › AROUND BRIDGETOWN

▲ Barbados Jazz Festival

Cool, mellow sounds float across the island for one week every January.

P.135 › ESSENTIALS

▶ Holders opera season

Classical music is not something you'll hear too often on a tropical island, but it's showcased wonderfully here.

P.88 › THE WEST COAST

Casual dining

Barbados has no lack of places catering for the well-to-do, but you don't have to be rolling in money to enjoy the island's culinary offerings. Delicious food at very reasonable prices can be found in many parts – though particularly in Bridgetown and along the south coast – from street vendors selling mouth-watering snacks to bustling markets and inexpensive restaurants and cafés.

▲ Vendors in St Lawrence Gap

Cheap and satisfying jerk chicken and other snacks fresh off the grill.

P.70 ▶ THE SOUTH COAST

▼ Fairchild Street Market

Come on Saturdays to see a mass of colourful produce turned out by smallholdings across the country.

P.57 ▶ BRIDGETOWN

◀ Back to Eden

This friendly place in Speightstown is an oasis for vegetarians in a country where meat and fish rule.

P.98 ▸ THE WEST COAST

▼ Indian Grill

Simple and delicious rotis stuffed with a variety of fillings; take one away and snack on the beach.

P.67 ▸ AROUND BRIDGETOWN

▲ Fisherman's Pub

Café, bar, music venue, tourist information centre – just a great all-round place to hang out.

P.99 ▸ THE WEST COAST

▼ Bay Garden

Don't miss a trip here for great atmosphere and some of the best fish on the island.

P.71 ▸ THE SOUTH COAST

Barbados wildlife

Most of Barbados's interesting wildlife can be found offshore, beneath the waves. Scuba-diving is, of course, the best way to see the reef fish, but snorkellers can spot some colourful coral, fish and turtles in shallow areas off the west coast.

On land, there's little by way of indigenous wildlife, but some species – like the island's canny green monkeys – have made their way here over the centuries, often as stowaways on sailing ships.

▲ Blue marlin

Go on a deep-sea fishing trip for a chance to hook the most magnificent of the billfish prowling the deep offshore waters.

P.139 ▸ ESSENTIALS

▲ Green monkeys

Visit the Barbados Wildlife Reserve to see these playful animals; just keep a tight grip on your handbag.

P.110 ▸ THE NORTH

▶ Hummingbirds

Tinier than you'd expect but surprisingly nifty, beating their wings up to seventy times a second.

P.121 ▶ THE EAST COAST

▲ Flying fish

They usually end up on dinner plates, but you may also see these amazing little fish in flight during a catamaran cruise.

P.134 ▶ ESSENTIALS

▼ Reef fish

Put your mask underwater and playful schools of these rainbow-coloured critters will soon swim past it.

P.92 ▶ THE WEST COAST

▼ Turtles

Prehistoric-looking, perhaps, but the most graceful creatures in the sea.

P.92 ▶ THE WEST COAST

Trips and tours

Not surprisingly, many of the numerous trips and tours offered in Barbados are water-based. All manner of craft will take you on, under or even over the ocean to fish, party or simply stare in awe at its beauty. And if this leaves you hungry for more, you can always check out how some of the neighbouring islands compare by taking a day trip to the Grenadines.

▲ Helicopter tour

A bit pricey, but these will be the best views that you'll ever get of Barbados.

P.129 › ESSENTIALS

▲ Atlantis Submarine

Dive beneath the waves for a close-up look at marine life that doesn't entail you getting wet.

P.138 › ESSENTIALS

▲ Charter boats for deep-sea fishing

Head out to sea to hunt down marlin, swordfish and barracuda on your own private charter.

P.139 ▸ ESSENTIALS

▶ Catamaran cruise

Whether you're after a party at sea or a quiet cruise, catamarans like *Silver Moon* are ready to weigh anchor.

P.138 ▸ ESSENTIALS

▼ Island-hopping

Escape to the Grenadine islands – if only for a day – for another taste of paradise.

P.129 ▸ ESSENTIALS

Places

Bridgetown

Located beside the strikingly beautiful white-sand beaches of Carlisle Bay, busy, modern Bridgetown is the capital (and only) city of Barbados. It's also one of the oldest urban centres in the Caribbean: the British settled here in 1628, around a protected inlet known as the Careenage; the area is still busy today, though mainly as a parking place for sleek yachts. Parliament, backed by a maze of narrow lanes marking the city's earliest sections, is just north of the waterfront, and the island's main religious buildings are within five minutes' walk of here. Visitors should note that there are no hotels in the city itself, and relatively few restaurants; the main tourist attractions are the duty-free shops and a couple of lively nightlife venues. Exploring the area on foot won't take more than half a day.

National Heroes Square

The capital's tiny main square, known for over a century as Trafalgar Square, was given its present name in 1999, though a bronze statue of Admiral Horatio Nelson is still its focal point. In the early nineteenth century, Barbados – like all the British West Indian islands – lived under threat of invasion by Napoleon's strong Caribbean-based navy. Admiral Nelson, commanding a British fleet in pursuit of the French, stopped briefly on the island in June 1805, just four months before he was killed at the Battle of Trafalgar. In honour

▲ THE CAREENAGE

of his visit, the Barbadian parliament granted funds for a statue by British sculptor Richard Westmacott, which was erected in 1813.

Getting there and around

Fast, efficient **buses** and **minibuses** run to the city from all over the island. If you're coming from the south coast, these pass through the Garrison area before terminating in the vicinity of the Fairchild Street Bus Station; the exact stop depends on whether you're on a government bus or one that is privately owned (see p.128). Coming from the west coast, most buses make their final stop near the corner of James and Tudor streets, just north of the city centre. If you're driving into Bridgetown, you'll have to negotiate a slightly tricky one-way street system, but there are plenty of safe, inexpensive areas in which to park right in the town centre. Once you're there, the central sights are most easily toured on foot.

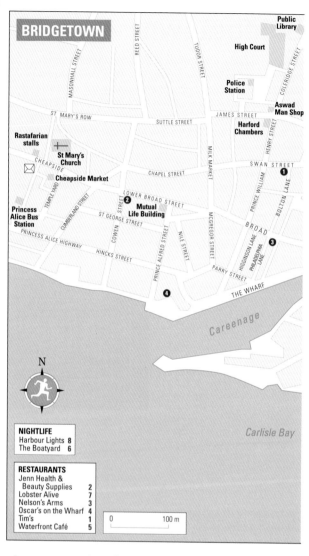

BRIDGETOWN

Public Library

High Court

Police Station

Aswad Man Shop

REED STREET

TUDOR STREET

COLERIDGE STREET

MASONHALL STREET

ST MARY'S ROW

SUTTLE STREET

JAMES STREET

Harford Chambers

HENRY STREET

Rastafarian stalls

St Mary's Church

CHEAPSIDE

MILK MARKET

SWAN STREET

PRINCE WILLIAM

BOLTON LANE

❶

CHAPEL STREET

Cheapside Market

LOWER BROAD STREET

❷

Mutual Life Building

TEMPLE YARD

CUMBERLAND STREET

ST GEORGE STREET

COWEN STREET

PRINCE ALFRED STREET

NILE STREET

McGREGOR STREET

B R O A D

HIGGINSON LANE

PHILADELPHIA LANE

❸

Princess Alice Bus Station

PRINCESS ALICE HIGHWAY

HINCKS STREET

PARRY STREET

THE WHARF

❹

Careenage

N

Carlisle Bay

NIGHTLIFE
Harbour Lights 8
The Boatyard 6

RESTAURANTS
Jenn Health & Beauty Supplies 2
Lobster Alive 7
Nelson's Arms 3
Oscar's on the Wharf 4
Tim's 1
Waterfront Café 5

0   100 m

In recent years, the awkward colonial connotations of the statue have caused much local controversy. Calypsonian Mighty Gabby scored a massive hit with his song *Take Down Nelson*, and there is ongoing talk of replacing Nelson's statue with one of a Bajan. Although an official decision to replace the statue has yet to be made, the government's declaration of ten National Heroes – among them cricketing genius Sir Garfield Sobers (who has his own grand bronze statue at

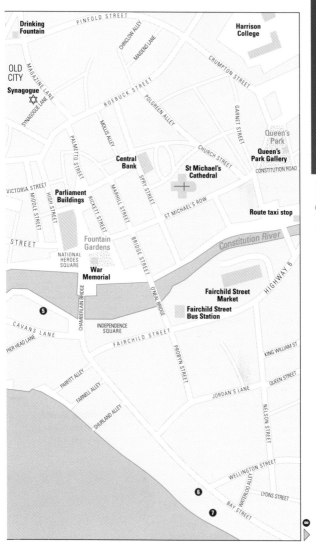

the entrance to town), slave leader Bussa (see box, p.82) and politicians Sir Grantley Adams and Errol Barrow – makes it seem likely that a statue of one of the ten will eventually replace Nelson in the square.

The war memorial and the Fountain Gardens

Immediately east of National Heroes Square, a simple, understated obelisk commemorates the Barbadians who died in World Wars I and II. During World War I, the War

▲ FOUNTAIN GARDENS

Office in London was reluctant to recruit black West Indians directly into British regiments. Instead, they established a separate British West Indies Regiment in 1915, which worked mainly in ammunition dumps and gun placements for the duration of the campaign. In World War II, the 1200-man-strong Caribbean Regiment was sent to Italy and then Egypt, but never saw action. Behind the memorial, the tiny, well-kept Fountain Gardens are home to an ornamental cascade, put up in 1865 to commemorate the introduction of piped water to the capital.

The Parliament Buildings

Opposite National Heroes Square. Open during parliamentary sessions only; for dates, visit Ⓦ www .barbadosparliament.com. The Parliament Buildings hold the island's two legislative houses, the assembly and the senate. Established in 1639, Barbados's Parliament is one of the oldest in the world. In its early years it met in a series of taverns and private homes, then moved in the eighteenth century to the building that now houses the High Court. Parliament's present Gothic Revival home, put up in the 1870s, features an arcaded courtyard and a church-like clock tower. If you're in town while Parliament is in session,

you are free to watch from the public gallery provided you're properly dressed (no shorts). Inside the debating chamber, on the upper floor of the east wing, a series of stained glass windows depicts thirteen British sovereigns, starting with James I, and including Oliver Cromwell and a very young Queen Victoria.

Harford Chambers

Corner of Prince William Henry and James streets. Immediately north of the earliest Parliament Buildings is the earliest part of the city, where the main roads are linked by small lanes and passageways. The area is home to one of Bridgetown's oldest surviving buildings, the pastel-pink Harford Chambers, whose irregular brickwork and Dutch gables are classic examples of seventeenth-century architecture. On the opposite corner, the **Aswad Man Shop** (which sells unremarkable clothes), with cast-iron balconies projecting over the pavement, dates from around 1840.

Along Coleridge Street

Heading north up Coleridge Street – a continuation of

▼ PARLIAMENT BUILDINGS

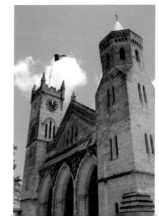

Prince William Henry Street – takes you past the gleaming white **police station** and the adjacent **High Court**, built in 1730 and originally home to the city's parliament and prison.

Next door is Bridgetown's imposing **public library** (Mon–Sat 9am–5pm), which proudly bears the words "Free Library" above its grand, columned entrance. The Barbados Parliament passed an act providing for a free library service in 1847, though this building – paid for by American philanthropist Andrew Carnegie – did not open until 1904. Across the road from the library stands an elaborate **drinking fountain**, a gift to the city from John Montefiore, one of its leading Jewish traders, in 1865. The fountain features stone reliefs of Prudence, Justice, Fortitude and Temperance, as well as exhortations to the thirsty citizens of Bridgetown to "Be sober minded" and "Look to the end".

The synagogue

Entrance on Synagogue Lane, just south of the drinking fountain. Daily 8.30am–4pm. Free. This pink-and-white edifice was first constructed in 1655, but had to be rebuilt after it was damaged by a hurricane in 1833. Jews were among the earliest settlers in Barbados; many of them arrived in the 1650s to escape the Inquisition in Brazil, bringing a knowledge of sugar-cane cultivation that later proved crucial in boosting the island's fledgling agriculture. Thirty years later, almost five percent of the island's population was Jewish, and many of the shops and businesses in the area around the synagogue were Jewish-

▲ ASWAD MAN SHOP

owned – Swan Street was once known as Jew Street.

By around 1900, though, a long-term decline in the sugar industry led much of the business class to emigrate, and the country's Jewish population shrank to fewer than twenty people. In 1929, its congregation reduced to just one person, the synagogue was sold to a private buyer and converted into offices. The government acquired it by compulsory purchase in 1983, with plans to demolish it and build a new Supreme Court on the site. However, a revitalized Jewish community – boosted during the 1930s and 1940s by refugees from Europe – persuaded the government to let them reclaim the building.

Backed by financial aid from Jewish groups overseas, extensive restoration has returned it to something like its original state. The attractive interior features replicas of the original glass chandeliers as well as a few authentic objects, including some cedarwood pews from 1834 and an old alms box. A series of newspaper articles displayed on the walls describes the restoration work and recounts some of the building's history. Anyone can enter the synagogue, although men must don one of the kipas provided in a basket at the entrance.

Outside, the Jewish cemetery is one of the oldest in the Western hemisphere, with dozens of cracked tombstones – some of them dating back to the seventeenth century – inscribed in Hebrew, English and Portuguese (a relic of settlers from Brazil).

St Michael's Cathedral

St Michael's Row. Daily 9am–4pm. Free. This large, red-roofed cathedral just east of the Parliament Buildings is the country's principal Anglican place of worship. A stone church was first erected here in 1665, but most of the present building dates from 1786; St Michael's was consecrated as a cathedral in 1825, when Barbados got

its first bishop. It's spacious and airy, with a large barrel roof and some fine mahogany carving in the pulpit and choir. A series of monumental sculptures decorate the walls – most notable is the relief in the choir dedicated to the city's first bishop, William Hart Coleridge – while the Lady Chapel, added in 1938 at the eastern end, is splashed with colour from its stained glass. The cathedral's sprawling churchyard is the resting-place for many of the island's most prominent figures, including the first premier Sir Grantley Adams and his son Tom Adams; if you're here in spring you may be lucky enough to catch the red frangipani trees in full bloom.

Central Bank

Spry Street. The nondescript modern building that towers

Bridgetown's bridges

Two **bridges** cross the Careenage, linking north and south Bridgetown. Nearest the sea, the pedestrian-only Chamberlain Bridge commemorates British Colonial Secretary Joseph Chamberlain's role in securing financial aid for the island's sugar industry in 1900. In front of the bridge stands the Independence Arch – erected in 1987 to celebrate the 21st birthday of Barbadian independence, it bears the national flag, motto and pledge of allegiance. A stone's throw away, the Charles Duncan O'Neal Bridge remembers the man who founded the country's first political party, the Democratic League, in 1924.

▲ CHAMBERLAIN BRIDGE

behind St Michael's Cathedral is the island's Central Bank: at eleven storeys, it's the tallest edifice in Barbados. It also holds the country's main performing-arts venue, **Frank Collymore Hall** (named after the great Barbadian poet, author, actor and journalist), which hosts lectures, seminars, concerts, film screenings and some of the events during Gospelfest (see p.135).

▲ MARKET PRODUCE

Queen's Park

Entrance on the corner of St Michael's Row and Crumpton Street. Queen's Park Gallery Mon–Sat 10am–6pm. Free. A couple of minutes' walk east of St Michael's Cathedral brings you to Queen's Park, a large open space that's a combination of public park and carefully tended sports pitches. Its main feature is the classically Georgian **Queen's Park Gallery** – built in 1783, it served as the residence for the general commanding the British armed forces in this part of the Caribbean until the British garrison left the island in 1905. Today it functions as an art gallery, featuring changing exhibitions (roughly every three weeks) of mostly local art, as well as occasionally hosting theatre performances. Standing in front of the house is an ancient baobab tree eighteen metres in circumference.

Fairchild Street Market

Fairchild Street, beside the bus concourse. Across the O'Neal Bridge from the Parliament Buildings, the Fairchild Street Market, on the left, is one of the city's two main food markets. Most of the trade is now done on the street in front of the market; only a few fruit and

vegetable stands are usually open inside the covered building. Saturday mornings are busiest: produce is brought in from around the island, making for a colourful – and photogenic – spectacle. There has been talk of the market being moved a few hundred metres down the street to the current location of the fire station, although at the time of writing, definite plans had yet to be announced.

Broad Street

Much of central Bridgetown is given over to shopping, with dozens of duty-free stores competing for the cruise ship dollar. Crossing back over the Careenage via the Chamberlain Bridge brings you to the start of the city's main drag, Broad Street – a duty-free paradise that runs west from National Heroes Square. The area has been the city's market centre since the mid-seventeenth century, and still retains some splendid colonial buildings amid the modern chaos of clothes shops,

▼ BROAD STREET

jewellery stores and fast-food joints. Halfway down the street, the enormous, late nineteenth-century **Mutual Life Building** (now occupied by Butterfield Bank), with its twin silver-domed towers and exquisite cast-iron fretwork, is the most distinctive of Bridgetown's colonial-era buildings.

St Mary's Church

At the western end of Broad Street.
Red-roofed St Mary's Church was built in 1827 on the site of the city's first church, which had been built around 1641 and named, like the present-day cathedral, St Michael's. It's a splendid piece of Georgian Neoclassicism, apart from the turreted tower that was tacked on several decades later. Sadly, the church is often locked, but the jalousied south porch and the shady graveyard are worth checking out. The cemetery is the final resting place of many Bajan luminaries, including Samuel Jackson Prescod (one of the National Heroes; see p.51) who was, in 1843, the first non-white elected to the national parliament. A large silk-cotton tree on the grounds of the

▼ ST MARY'S CHURCH

church, known as the "Justice Tree", was once the site of public hangings.

Cheapside

West of St Mary's Church, Broad Street turns into Cheapside, where you'll find the Princess Alice Bus Station (for buses and minibuses heading to points north and west), as well as the General Post Office and the city's other main market, Cheapside Market. Just before the market, Temple Street runs down to the waterfront. This area, known as **Temple Yard**, takes its name from an early nineteenth-century **Masonic Lodge**, or temple, used by the Order of the Ancient Masons until it was destroyed by a hurricane in 1831. The city's Rastafarians used to operate stalls here; they and their wares – sandals and other hand-crafted leather goods, as well as their distinctive red, gold and green jewellery and headgear – have now moved to a new location directly opposite the General Post Office.

Pelican Craft Centre

Immediately west of the Princess Alice Bus Station ☎ 426 0765. Most shops Mon–Fri 9am–5pm, Sat 9am–2pm.
The Pelican Craft Centre is an excellent shopping complex. Built on reclaimed land, it features a small art gallery, thirty or so shops selling some of the more interesting and better quality souvenirs around – from locally produced skin-care products to pottery and metalwork – and a snack bar that offers such Bajan specialities as cou-cou and, on Saturdays, pudding and souse. Within the complex, you can watch cigars being rolled at the **Caribbean Cigar Company** (Mon–Thurs

8am–4.30pm, Fri 8am–4pm), and potters and wood-turners hard at work in their small studios at the western end of the building.

Shops

Cave Shepherd

Broad Street, opposite *Nelson's Arms* ☏ 227 2121. Mon–Thurs 8.30am–5.30pm, Fri 8.30am–6.30pm, Sat 8.30am–4pm. Duty-free shopping doesn't get any better than at Cave Shepherd. A good selection of low-cost tobacco, alcohol and perfume products, plus everything else you could ever want, from sunglasses to rum cake. You need to bring your passport and return ticket or departure card to get the duty-free prices.

The Clay Gallery

Pelican Craft Centre, in the Indigenous Potteries workshop ☏ 431 0747. Mon–Fri 9am–5pm, Sat 9am–2pm. If you can't make it up to Chalky Mount (see p.107), this is a good place to buy monkey jugs and other pottery done in the old Bajan style. The store doubles as a workshop where you can watch pieces being made.

Earth Mother Botanicals

Pelican Craft Centre ☏ 228 2743. Mon–Fri 9am–5pm, Sat 9am–2pm. All of the skin-care products here are made with Barbadian herbs, flowers and fruits, making for some original gift ideas, such as sugar-cane body scrub and spicy rum aftershave.

Harrisons

Broad Street, opposite Cave Shepherd ☏ 431 5550. Mon–Fri 9am–5.30pm, Sat 9am–4pm. If the Cave Shepherd duty-free shops haven't got what you're looking for, try here.

Little Switzerland

DaCostas Mall, Broad Street ☏ 431 0030. Mon–Thurs 9am–5pm, Fri 9am–6pm, Sat 9am–3pm. Though Little Switzerland specialises in designer watches, window-shoppers should take a look at the stunning hand-made gemstone globes in the back of the shop.

Restaurants

Jenn Health & Beauty Supplies

Corner of Lower Broad and Cowell streets ☏ 426 1276. Mon–Thurs 8.30am–5pm, Fri 8.30am–6pm, Sat 8.30am–3pm. This shop sells herbal remedies and other health-promoting products, so its snack bar is perfect for a quick and nutritious bite to eat. Choices include fresh tuna sandwiches (B$6), okra, yam and other vegetarian dishes for around B$3 per portion, and refreshing energy shakes and smoothies for around B$6.

Lobster Alive

Bay Street, next to *The Boatyard* ☏ 435 0305. Lunch Mon–Sat noon–4pm, dinner daily 6–9pm. Popular spot serving delicious seafood in a lovely beachside setting. Most people come for the lobsters, which you can pick from the tank and have cooked to order (B$115 for a medium serving), but other things are good too – try the conch samosas (B$25) or fish, shrimp and steak main courses (B$40-55). Enjoy live jazz performances on Tuesday evenings and during Sunday lunch.

Nelson's Arms

Galleria Mall, 27 Broad Street ☏ 431 0602. Mon–Fri 8am–7pm, Sat 8am–5pm. Busy pub in the heart of duty-free shopping land

▲ THE WATERFRONT CAFÉ

– nautically themed and suitably decorated with sailors and pirates – that makes for a decent lunch break, with flying fish, chicken and pasta (B$15–25) served on a first-floor balcony overlooking Broad Street.

Oscar's on the Wharf

Carlisle Wharf ☎ 427 0017. Mon–Thurs 8am–7pm, Fri 8am–midnight, Sat 8am–3am. Located where the Careenage meets the sea, *Oscar's* is the perfect place to enjoy a drink or a slice of cake while you watch the boats pass by. The menu is somewhat limited, although the kingfish steaks and blackened shrimp (B$35) are good value.

Tim's

Corner of Bolton Lane and Swan Street ☎ 228 0645. Mon–Sat 7.30–10.30am & 11am–3pm. Choose what you want from a buffet of Bajan staples – peas and rice, macaroni pie and flying fish, to name but a few – at this popular and informal lunch spot, then eat your meal either in the air-conditioned dining room or on the little balcony overlooking pedestrian-only Swan Street. A full lunch including meat or fish costs around B$15.

The Waterfront Café

The Careenage ☎ 427 0093. Mon–Sat 10am–3pm & 6–10pm. Some of the best food in Bridgetown, with an authentic Caribbean flavour, and a lovely ambience to match, especially if you choose to eat outside in front of the yachts moored in the Careenage. Try the excellent snapper, flying fish (served with cou-cou) or dolphin fish – from B$38 to B$59 – or, if you just want a snack, the bol jol (cod with lime), soups and salads. There's live music most evenings, normally steel pan (Tues) and jazz (Wed, Fri & Sat). No cover charge.

Nightlife

The Boatyard

Bay Street ☎ 436 2622. Daily 8am–2am. This sprawling beachclub featuring both day- and night-time entertainment is one of the island's best known. Tuesday is the most popular night, when there's live music and unlimited drinks for B$35. Saturday follows a similar all-you-can-drink format, but without the band, for B$25. During the day you can lounge around on the beach or play volleyball. The decent selection of food includes grilled fish, burgers and pasta, with most dishes costing around B$20–30.

Harbour Lights

Bay Street ☎ 436 7225. Daily 9pm–2am. Smaller version of *The Boatyard*, with a friendly atmosphere and a similar programme of all-you-can-drink beach parties for B$40–45. On Mondays and Wednesdays the drinks come with a Bajan dinner, live music, limbo dancing, fire-eating and acrobatic performances for B$115, which also includes free transport back to your hotel after you've drunk the place dry.

Around Bridgetown

Once you've had your fill of the capital – which won't take too long – it's worth investigating some of the sights around Bridgetown; most of the choice ones fall within a couple of kilometres of the city centre. To the south is the historic Garrison area, where the British empire maintained its Caribbean military headquarters from 1780 to 1905. Chock full of superb Georgian architecture, it remains one of Bridgetown's most evocative districts and retains many of the island's attractive colonial military buildings. To the north, much of the area around the Kensington Oval, the island's principal cricket ground, is given over to industrial production, including a couple of rum factories that are open for tours, while to the north-east is Tyrol Cot, the former home of the island's first premier, Sir Grantley Adams.

Garrison Savannah

The centre of the Garrison area, just a couple of kilometres south of the city centre, is the savannah, a huge grassy space that once served as the army's parade ground. The military buildings – barracks, quartermaster's store and hospitals, as well as the fort itself – stand in a rough square around its outer edges, flanked by coconut palms and large mango trees. Between the savannah and Bay Street stands the spectacular **Main Guard** with its tall, bright red tower and green cupola. Across the

▲ MAIN GUARD, GARRISON SAVANNAH

road you can see the thick eighteenth-century walls of **St Ann's Fort** (now used by the Barbados Defence Force and closed to visitors), surrounded by ranks of ancient but well-preserved black iron

Getting there and around

If you're coming to the Garrison area from the west coast, catch a **bus** or **minibus** heading for the south coast via the Garrison (for example, the Speightstown-to-Oistins government bus); buses marked Bridgetown stop in the city centre, a couple of kilometres short of the Garrison area. From the south coast, all buses and **route taxis** going to the capital will stop by the Garrison Savannah; and, conversely, all buses leaving Bridgetown's Fairchild Street Bus Station for the south coast will pass the Garrison. Walking from Bridgetown centre to the Kensington Oval will take around twenty minutes; Tyrol Cot and the rum factories are best visited with your own transport or a taxi.

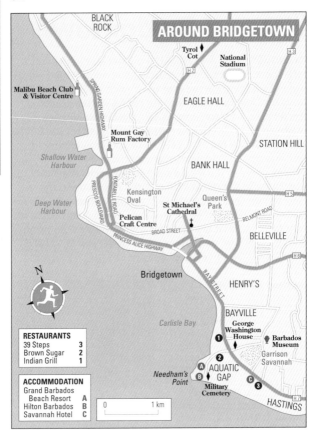

AROUND BRIDGETOWN

BLACK ROCK

Tyrol Cot

National Stadium

Malibu Beach Club & Visitor Centre

EAGLE HALL

Mount Gay Rum Factory

STATION HILL

Shallow Water Harbour

BANK HALL

Deep Water Harbour

Kensington Oval

Queen's Park

St Michael's Cathedral

BELMONT ROAD

BELLEVILLE

Pelican Craft Centre

BROAD STREET

PRINCESS ALICE HIGHWAY

SPRING GARDEN HIGHWAY

FONTABELLE ROAD

PRESCOD BOULEVARD

BAY STREET

Bridgetown

HENRY'S

N

BAYVILLE

Carlisle Bay

George Washington House

Barbados Museum

Garrison Savannah

❶

Needham's Point

❷

AQUATIC GAP

A

B

Military Cemetery

C

❸

HASTINGS

RESTAURANTS

39 Steps	3
Brown Sugar	2
Indian Grill	1

ACCOMMODATION

Grand Barbados Beach Resort	A
Hilton Barbados	B
Savannah Hotel	C

0   1 km

cannons pointing menacingly across the savannah. The savannah itself is still quite active, with sports grounds and play areas bounded by the city's **racetrack**, which sees action several times a year, particularly during the island's Gold Cup horse race in March (for dates of all race meets, call ☏426 3980 or visit ⓦwww .barbadosturfclub.com). On Independence Day (Nov 30), the island's forces – the Coast Guard, the Barbados Defence Force and the younger cadets – maintain tradition by parading

on the savannah in front of the island's governor-general.

Barbados Museum

St Ann's Garrison ☏427 0201, ⓦwww.barbmuse.org.bb. Mon–Sat 9am–5pm, Sun 2–6pm. B$11.50. Housed in the Garrison's old military prison on the east side of the savannah, this worthwhile museum is stuffed with interesting and informative exhibits on the island's history and culture. A series of galleries run clockwise around an airy central courtyard that once rang with the sound of prisoners breaking stones. Indeed, one of the museum's best features is the chance to look inside one of the spartan prison cells, where iron rings in the walls where the beds were hung are hardly wide enough apart for a baby, let alone a full-grown man.

Be sure to check out two of the museum's more recent acquisitions, positioned at the building's entrance, both of which are reminders of the country's unsavoury colonial past: an 1834 plantation deed that lists the slaves considered to be part of the estate's property, and a sinister-looking "collar" once used to punish disobedient workers.

The first gallery inside the entrance chronicles the history of Barbados's earliest inhabitants, the Amerindians – the immaculate little shell carving of a human figure, dating from 1000 to 1500 AD, is a highlight. Subsequent galleries go on to trace the country's evolution from a sugar-based slave society through emancipation and the early struggles of the majority black population to today's democratic, independent nation.

The rest of the museum is given over to exhibits on local flora and fauna, military artefacts, and prints and paintings of old Barbados and African crafts, the latter put into context by displays on the continent's history and geography. There is also no shortage of antique furniture – notably a locally made 1830s four-poster mahogany bed – ceramics and other such items, showcased nicely in a replica bedroom, dining room, living

▲ MILITARY HOSPITAL, GARRISON AREA

room and nursery of an old plantation house.

George Washington House

Bush Hill, on the north side of the Garrison Savannah ☎ 228 5461, ⓦ www.georgewashingtonbarbados .org. Mon–Sat 9am–5pm. B$25. This red-roofed house (also known as Bush Hill House) is where George Washington lodged for seven weeks during a visit to the island in 1751. Although he contracted smallpox during his stay, the future first American president was full of praise for Bajan hospitality. The illness may have been a blessing in disguise, as the immunity that he gained protected him from the smallpox epidemic that destroyed parts of the Continental army during the American Revolution. The house has been completely restored and is now open as a museum. After watching a fifteen-minute video intended to set the scene for Washington's arrival in Barbados, you are taken on a tour of the ground floor of the house, which has been made to look like it did in 1751. The first floor contains displays focusing on the link

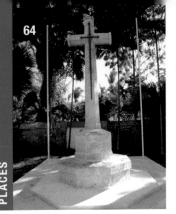

▲ MILITARY CEMETERY, NEEDHAM'S POINT

between the US and Barbados, as well as life in general on the island during the eighteenth century – nothing much that you won't already have seen if you've stopped at the Barbados Museum.

Aquatic Gap and Needham's Point

If you rejoin Bay Street at Bush Hill and head away from Bridgetown, the first turn on the right takes you through Aquatic Gap – home to several expensive hotels and restaurants – to the tiny peninsula of Needham's Point. One of the earliest British colonial fortresses, Fort Charles, was built on this spit of land in the 1660s. Though it fell into ruin long ago, parts of the old walls were incorporated into the grounds of the *Hilton Barbados* (see p.67), which, together with a large oil refinery, takes up most of the peninsula and overlooks a pleasant, bustling white-sand beach popular with families at weekends. Next to the refinery and signposted as you drive up to the *Hilton* is a **military cemetery** (daily 6am–6pm; free) dedicated to the British troops who died on duty in the colony. Barbadians who died in World Wars I and II are

also commemorated in several memorials.

Kensington Oval

Northern outskirts of Bridgetown. Ticket and schedule information at ☎ 436 1397. The Kensington Oval is the island's premier **cricket** ground and venue for international test matches. To reach the stadium, head northwest on Fontabelle Road towards the city's shallow harbour and take the signposted right turn just before the top of the road.

At the time of writing, Kensington Oval was being completely overhauled in preparation for the 2007 Cricket World Cup, and was subsequently closed to the public. When it re-opens, expect a state-of-the-art stadium, complete with a 16,000-capacity main stand (one of the largest in the cricketing world; the total ground capacity will be 28,000, making the Kensington Oval the largest cricket stadium in the West Indies) and another, five-storey stand named after Barbadian batsman George Challenor, which will be the second highest building in Bridgetown after the Central Bank (see p.56). For more on the game of cricket, see p.141.

Mount Gay Rum Factory

Spring Garden Highway ☎ 425 8757, ⓦ www.mountgayrum.com. Mon–Fri 9am–4pm, 45min tours at half past every hour. B$12. This place offers marginally the better of the factory tours available in the area. Visits start with a short film giving the history of the company, which first distilled rum on the island in 1703 and is reckoned to be the world's oldest surviving producer of the spirit. Although Mount Gay Rum is actually distilled at the company's factory in the northern parish of St Lucy, the tour shows you all the later stages in the production process, including refining, ageing, blending and bottling. The highlight of the tour is probably the vast, cool storage area, which is crammed with barrels oozing the sweet, heady smell of rum, and where the "angel's share" of evaporated rum drips from the ceiling. At the end of the circuit, visitors can head to the bar, where the barman demonstrates how to be a rum-taster, and offers a complimentary cocktail – sit outside and enjoy it on the veranda overlooking the attractively landscaped gardens. There's also a small shop that sells the distillery's products (although you'll find them cheaper at supermarkets or the duty-free shops in town), as well as assorted T-shirts and other paraphernalia.

Malibu Beach Club & Visitor Centre

Spring Garden Highway ☏ 425 9393. Mon–Fri 9–11am & noon–4pm, tours every 30min. B$20. The other rum tour in the area is at the Malibu Beach Club & Visitor Centre,

adjoining the West India Rum Distillery. All of Malibu's world-famous coconut-flavoured white rum (and the less well-known lime-flavoured stuff) is manufactured here, and you get pretty much the same tour as at Mount Gay, though there isn't quite the same sense of history. The factory, right on the edge of the sea, has beautiful views of the turquoise water below from the distilling tanks on the upper deck of the building. After the tour, retire to the little stretch of sand at the Malibu Beach Club and kick back in a lounge chair (included in the tour price) with a complimentary cocktail.

Tyrol Cot

Codrington Hill ☏ 424 2074. Mon–Fri 8am–4pm. B$14. The exquisite little house of Tyrol Cot, three kilometres or so from Bridgetown centre, was the launch pad for two of the island's most illustrious political careers. Sir Grantley Adams, the first elected leader of pre-independence Barbados, lived here, as did his son, Tom Adams (who was born in the house), the nation's prime minister from

▲ COCKTAILS BENEATH PALMS

PLACES Around Bridgetown

Making and drinking rum

Rum has been a key part of Barbadian life for over three centuries, so there's really no better place to acquire a taste for the stuff. Made infamous by its status as the favourite drink of pirates and as "grog", dished out to sailors in the British navy to keep them from mutiny, rum is the most potent by-product of sugar, which has been grown all over the island since the 1640s.

It takes ten to twelve tonnes of sugar cane to produce just half a bottle of rum. Though production is now mechanized, the basic distilling method hasn't changed much over the centuries. To start, sugar cane juice is extracted, boiled and put through a centrifuge to make thick, sticky molasses. This is then diluted with water, and yeast is added to get the mix fermenting. After fermentation, the concoction is heated, and the evaporating alcohol captured in holding tanks.

In rum shops across the island, small knots of men (and occasionally women) prop up the bar beside a bottle of cheap white rum and a bottle of water, mixing their drinks to the desired strength. The choice of drink is a fine art, with a variety of bottle sizes – miniature, mini, flask, quart and pint in ascending order of size – and an equally varied selection of rums. White rum is the basis of most rum cocktails, although there are several richer, mellower options, from the golden rums of Cockspur and Mount Gay to the latter's fabulous Extra Old dark rum, best drunk neat over ice. Their darker colour is acquired from the charred American oak barrels in which they are left to mature.

For more information on the making and drinking of rum, check out the Mount Gay Rum Factory website, Ⓦ www.mountgayrum.com

1976 until his death in 1985. The single-storey, coral-block house was built in 1854 by William Farnum, one of the island's leading architects, and combines classic European and vernacular Caribbean styles. The Demerara windows, for example, are framed by Roman arches but contain adjustable double-jalousied shutters, with sloping slats that keep out rain and sun but let in light and allow air to circulate. Each of the windows also has a small but intricate cast-iron guard at its base, a flamboyant, if rather eccentric, addition. Inside, a collection of the family's belongings includes an antiquated computer used by Tom, various mahogany antiques and Sir Grantley's personal effects – among them the flag of his political dream, the Federation of the West Indies, of which he was the first and only prime minister.

A tiny heritage village, featuring half a dozen old-fashioned chattel houses, has been built outside the house. The interiors of three of these structures are designed to show how a chattel house, a slave hut and a blacksmith's workshop would have looked back in the 1930s, while inside the other buildings local potters, artists and basket-makers sell their wares (and occasionally demonstrate their trades). There's also a typical Barbadian rum shop where you can get a drink and a bite to eat.

Accommodation

Grand Barbados Beach Resort

Aquatic Gap ☎ 426 4000, ℗ 429 2400, Ⓦ www.grandbarbados .com. The opening of the *Hilton* in Needham's Point has overshadowed what was previously the island's premier hotel for business travellers. The 130-plus rooms (from US$188/168 in winter/summer) are somewhat impersonal, but do all have balconies. Facilities include a gym, a modest pool and an adequate beach – though the rather monstrous pier jutting off it somewhat mars the view.

Hilton Barbados

Needham's Point ☎ 426 0200, 🖷 434 5770, ⓦ www.hiltoncaribbean.com/barbados. Dominating the tip of the peninsula, this impressive 350-room hotel caters equally to those visiting on business or pleasure, combining conference rooms and exhibition centres with two secluded beaches, tennis courts and a labyrinthine pool that weaves through the attractive grounds. All of the brightly coloured rooms (US$450/210 in winter/summer) have balconies with ocean views.

Savannah Hotel

Hastings, just south of the Garrison Savannah ☎ 228 3800, 🖷 228 4385, ⓦ www.gemsbarbados.com. A well-designed complex a short walk from the beach, where some of the one hundred elegantly furnished rooms, complete with four-poster beds, are housed in the historic and newly renovated buildings of the Garrison. The staff is friendly and helpful, and amenities include two big pools, two restaurants and a fitness centre. Rooms from US$327/266 in winter/summer.

Restaurants

39 Steps

Chattel Plaza, Hastings, just south of the Garrison Savannah ☎ 427 0715. Mon–Fri noon–3pm & 6.30pm–midnight, Sat 6.30pm–midnight. Fashionable and convivial wine bar and restaurant; the daily specials normally include several excellent fish dishes (B$30–55), as well as good soups and salads. Mellow live jazz on some Saturdays.

Brown Sugar

Aquatic Gap ☎ 426 7684. Daily noon–2.30pm & 6–9.30pm, closed Sat lunch & Sun dinner. Housed in an attractive little building with iron fretwork and draped with greenery inside, this cosy place serves the best food in the Garrison area – the seafood, which includes plantain-crusted mahi mahi and the "Oistins Choice", a selection of fish, is particularly good. There's also a whopping buffet lunch for B$45 (Mon–Fri) or B$55 on Sundays, when steel pan music accompanies the eating. Dinner prices start around B$35 (B$50 for seafood).

Indian Grill

Bayside Plaza, Bay Street; just north of the Garrison Savannah ☎ 436 2361. Mon–Sat 11am–4pm. *Indian Grill* dishes up huge, delicious rotis stuffed with chicken, shrimp and vegetables, all with an East-Indian flavour (B$8–12). There are also daily specials, such as chicken curry and dhal, for around B$10.

The south coast

The parish of Christ Church, in the south of the island, was the birthplace of tourism in Barbados, and it remains dominated by the trappings of the holiday industry. The main highway here hugs the coast, linking a string of small resorts; each consists of a fringe of white-sand beach backed by a cluster of hotels, restaurants and tourist facilities. On the whole, the area is not as beautiful as the west coast, nor as lorded over by the staggering palaces of the mega-rich, but the beaches are just as fine, there are plenty of good restaurants and prices are much more reasonable.

Hastings

A five-minute bus ride east of Bridgetown is Hastings, which first developed in the eighteenth century as a by-product of Britain's military development of the nearby Garrison area (see p.61). Soldiers from St Ann's Fort were quartered here – you can still see their red-brick barracks on your left as you enter the town – and a naval hospital and the Admiral's quarters were built to the south along the coast. More than a century later, its proximity to the capital led Hastings to develop as Barbados's first tourist resort, and a handful of grand old hotels on the seafront still mark those glory days. Sadly, the once-attractive beach has been heavily eroded, but recent development has reinvigorated the area, adding a fresh splash of colour and new life.

Rockley

As you continue east, Hastings merges into the next village along the coast, the tiny tourist centre of Rockley. The beach here – known locally as **Accra Beach** – is magnificent; a great white swathe of sand, it's popular with both visitors and locals, and can get pretty crowded during the peak season and on weekends. The people-watching is top-notch, as hair-braiders, T-shirt and craft vendors and the odd hustler coexist with windsurfers and sun-ripening tourists to create one of the liveliest beach scenes on the island. Behind the beach

---

Getting there and around

Getting to and around the south coast is a breeze. Frequent **buses** and **minibuses** run east from Bridgetown, passing through most of the tourist zones along the water, and **route taxis** go as far east as Silver Sands. Service stops around midnight, though, so you'll need a car or a private taxi after that. Getting here directly from the west coast can be a little tricky – buses run between Speightstown and Oistins, usually bypassing Bridgetown, though they're less frequent than the ones that ply the south coast. When returning to the south coast from Bridgetown, try to avoid the late afternoon, as buses are invariably packed and waits at the numerous traffic lights around the Garrison area can be long.

▲ HAIR-BRAIDING STALL, ACCRA BEACH

are a couple of decent places to stay, though much of the main highway that runs through Rockley has been given over to slightly garish fast-food joints that reek of over-development. Higher up, away from the beach and rarely seen by tourists, are some of the island's most exclusive residential districts, home to bankers, lawyers and other professionals working in Bridgetown.

Worthing

Like the English seaside resort for which it is named, the once-elegant village of Worthing is now tatty and faded, but its easygoing feel and handful of decent, inexpensive guesthouses make it a popular destination for budget travellers. There's a gleaming white beach, less crowded than Accra Beach to the west but just as enjoyable, with a laid-back bar, several T-shirt vendors and locals offering boat trips and jet-ski rentals. St Lawrence Gap, just five minutes' walk away, offers more in the way of restaurants and nightlife, but Worthing is a pleasant alternative if you want to escape the crowds. Highway 7 runs through the village, with a string of shops, banks and supermarkets on its north side and all of the accommodation to the south.

Graeme Hall Nature Sanctuary

Worthing, 200m before the turn-off to St Lawrence Gap ☎ 435 9727 or 435 7078, ⊛ www.graemehall.com. Daily 8am–6pm. B$25. The focal point of this nature sanctuary is **Graeme Hall Swamp**. One of the few remaining mangrove swamps on the island, it's an important ecosystem that provides shelter for several species of fish and migratory birds. Boardwalks bring you close enough to the brackish waters to give you a good look at the mangroves and their huge aerial roots, while a couple of observation huts are the best place for bird-watching; expect to see several varieties of heron, egret and tern, among others. Two large, attractively designed aviaries provide additional opportunities for looking at parrots and several different types of wading birds, including flamingos and scarlet ibis.

Harry Bayley Observatory

Clapham, just south of Highway 6 ☎ 426-1317. Viewings every Fri at 9pm, depending on the weather. B$10. Stargazers should head north of Worthing to Harry Bayley Observatory. Built in 1963, it's still one of the more technologically advanced of the few observatories that exist in the West Indies. The Barbados Astronomical Society uses the building as its headquarters, and opens it to the public on Friday evenings. The first quarter of the month, when there is very little moonlight, is the best time

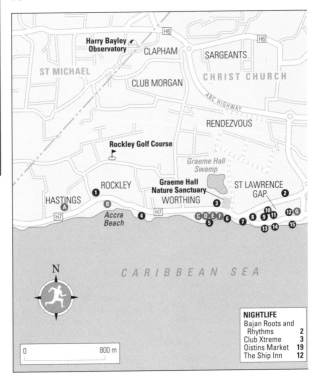

NIGHTLIFE
Bajan Roots and
  Rhythms   2
Club Xtreme   3
Oistins Market   19
The Ship Inn   12

to plan a visit, as you will be able to see the most stars. If the weather is at all questionable (for instance, very cloudy or threatening to rain), call ahead to confirm that the observatory is open.

St Lawrence Gap and Dover

With hotels, restaurants and tourist shops strung out along virtually the entire road, St

▼ FOOTBALL FIELD, DOVER

Lawrence Gap and the adjacent village of Dover, the next points east of Worthing along Highway 7, are something of a tourist enclave; you'll see few Bajans here, other than those who work in the industry or as street vendors. Still, despite all the hubbub, it remains a laid-back place with great beaches, particularly towards the eastern end of St Lawrence Gap. The south coast buses and minibuses will drop you on Highway 7 by the entrance to St Lawrence Gap; from here you'll have to continue on foot through the Gap itself to Dover (about fifteen minutes).

Maxwell

Continuing east on Highway 7 past the roundabout, it's easy to

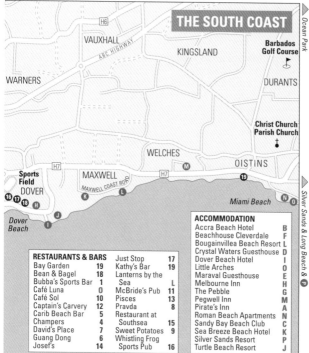

THE SOUTH COAST

VAUXHALL

ABC HIGHWAY

H6

KINGSLAND

Barbados
Golf Course

WARNERS

DURANTS

Christ Church
Parish Church

WELCHES

OISTINS

Sports
Field

MAXWELL

H7

DOVER

MAXWELL COAST ROAD

Miami Beach

Dover
Beach

ACCOMMODATION

Accra Beach Hotel	B
Beachhouse Cleverdale	F
Bougainvillea Beach Resort	L
Crystal Waters Guesthouse	D
Dover Beach Hotel	I
Little Arches	O
Maraval Guesthouse	E
Melbourne Inn	H
The Pebble	G
Pegwell Inn	M
Pirate's Inn	A
Roman Beach Apartments	N
Sandy Bay Beach Club	C
Sea Breeze Beach Hotel	K
Silver Sands Resort	P
Turtle Beach Resort	J

RESTAURANTS & BARS

Bay Garden	19	Just Stop	17
Bean & Bagel	18	Kathy's Bar	19
Bubba's Sports Bar	1	Lanterns by the	
Café Luna	O	Sea	L
Café Sol	10	McBride's Pub	11
Captain's Carvery	12	Pisces	13
Carib Beach Bar	5	Pravda	8
Champers	4	Restaurant at	
David's Place	7	Southsea	15
Guang Dong	6	Sweet Potatoes	9
Josef's	14	Whistling Frog	
		Sports Pub	16

drive straight through Maxwell
without noticing it. It's not a bad
choice as a place to stay, though,
with a couple of good hotels
just to the south on the Maxwell
Coast Road, a small loop off
the main drag. The beaches
here are as good as those to
the west, although there's less
sense of community and the
area can feel rather isolated in
the evenings. It's a popular place
with windsurfers, particularly
beginners and intermediates;
experts tend to head east for the
more challenging conditions at
Silver Sands (see p.73).

Oistins

Just east of Maxwell is Oistins
(the unusual name is a
corruption of "Austin", one

of the first landowners in the
area), the most built-up town
along the south coast, but
not a place visited much by
tourists, although it is linked to
Bridgetown by frequent buses,
as well as route taxi #11, which
continues to Silver Sands. The
busy little town is dominated
by a central fish market that
retains a sense of Barbados
before the tourist boom, and
Oistins' fishing tradition is
celebrated at the annual Oistins
Fish Festival every March. The
best time to visit the market is
in the evening, when a dozen
small shacks in the **Bay Garden**
eating area (see p.76) sell fried
fish straight from the boats.
On Friday nights hundreds of
people descend for a "lime", the

local term for a social gathering (for more on Friday nights at Oistins, see p.79).

Christ Church Parish Church

Church Hill. Daily 9am–5pm. Free.
Highway 7 continues east after Oistins, but the main road veers inland and climbs up the hill to join Highway 6, passing spooky Christ Church Parish Church on the way. The present squat, turreted coral building is the church's fifth incarnation, the others having been destroyed by various fires and hurricanes. Inside, there's a modern stained-glass window behind the altar, a series of plaster reliefs along the walls and an attractive mahogany gallery at the back. The sprawling cemetery that surrounds the church is also worth a look, with plenty of intriguing, crumbling tombs amid the frangipani and sago palms. The history of the Chase family vault, on the church's south side, is quite peculiar: three times during the early nineteenth century the vault was opened for a new burial, only to reveal that the lead coffins had mysteriously shifted from their original positions. When this happened a fourth time, after the vault had been officially locked under the governor's seal, the coffins were taken out and buried elsewhere in the churchyard.

Ocean Park

Balls Complex, Balls ☎ 420 7405, ⒲ www.oceanparkbarbados.com. Daily 9am–6pm. B$35, miniature golf B$5 extra. Continue up the hill from Christ Church Parish Church, and just past the roundabout on the left you'll find the island's newest attraction. A combination of indoor aquariums and outdoor displays, Ocean Park covers the whole gamut of marine life, from sea urchins to nurse sharks and barracudas. There is also a ray pool and a rehabilitation centre for rescued creatures, although on the whole there is disappointingly little in the way of unusual or eye-catching animals to justify the

Chattel houses

In the nineteenth century, most of tiny Barbados was given over to sugar production, and the island's poor, landless workers were forced to eke out tenuous existences on their employers' plantations. Forever at risk of being evicted – in which case they would lose their homes – the workers devised mobile homes that could be taken to pieces and rebuilt elsewhere if need be. Taking their name from the legal term "chattel", meaning a moveable possession, these houses were originally built from planks of cheap pine, imported from North America in pre-cut lengths, and placed on a foundation of limestone blocks. The facades were symmetrical, with a central door flanked by two windows; the roof was steeply gabled and the windows were jalousied to allow air to circulate and to give the house stability during hurricanes. The interiors were small, usually divided into two rooms, but as the owners earned money, they would take the back off the house to add an identical unit, a shed with a flat roof or a small veranda in the front. Owners with an artistic inclination (and the cash) would add fretwork over the doors and windows and maybe a hood above the window to keep rain out.

Few new **chattel houses** are built today, although plenty of people still live in existing ones. Their attractive design has remained popular and their influence can be seen in larger houses in affluent areas of Bridgetown and in tourist bars and shopping centres across the island.

high entrance price. A pirate-themed miniature golf course provides further entertainment, particularly for kids.

Miami Beach

To get to Miami Beach, head east from Oistins on Highway 7, take the right hand turn-off for Enterprise (a tiny village), and then turn right again at the Enterprise Coast Road, which offers a fabulous drive beside the sea. Upon reaching the coastal road, make one more right towards the beach – a lovely stretch dotted with casuarina trees that marks the last protected bathing area before you round the headland to the exposed south-central and southeastern beaches. You'll often find local Bajans exercising here, children playing cricket on the beach and elderly folk taking a refreshing morning swim. Alternatively, turn left past the South Point lighthouse for Silver Sands and Long Beach.

Silver Sands and Long Beach

Famous for its windsurfing, Silver Sands attracts enthusiasts from all over the world, though you'll find non-surfers here too, enjoying the village's quiet, easy-going vibe. The winds blow consistently for most of the year and there are a handful of (pretty expensive) places where you can rent a windsurfer if you haven't brought your own; try Club Mistral at the *Silver Sands Hotel* (☎ 428 6001). The beaches here are less busy than those to the west – mainly because of the often choppy seas – but equally attractive: true to its name, Long Beach, just beyond the *Ocean Spray Apartments*, is the longest beach on the island. A huge stretch of crunchy white sand strewn with driftwood, it is often completely deserted.

Shops

The Kandy Store

Chattel House Village, St Lawrence Gap ☎ 418 7399. Mon 1–6pm, Tues–Sat 10am–6pm. Hidden by several shops selling the usual tourist souvenirs, this discreet sex shop is one of only two on the whole island. There is no pornography, but the selection of sexy board games and various intimate gadgets could be a lifesaver for honeymooning couples.

Wine World

Rockley ☎ 435 8523. Mon–Thurs 9am–5pm, Fri 9am–6pm, Sat 9am–2pm. If you're looking for a vintage bottle of Bordeaux, this is where you'll find it. Prices, however, are steep; wine and spirits are generally sold for less at supermarkets. Other locations in Bridgetown, Holetown and Warrens.

Accommodation

Accra Beach Hotel

Rockley ☎ 435 8920, ⊕ 435 6794, ⓦ www.accrabeachhotel.com. Large, attractive hotel with 146 pleasant rooms right on the island's busiest beach, featuring balconies overlooking the sea,

▼ SILVER SANDS

palm-tree-shaded gardens and a giant swimming pool. Come evening there's a Polynesian restaurant and an outdoor dance floor. Rooms from US$191/154 in winter/summer.

Beachhouse Cleverdale

Worthing ☏ 428 1035, ℻ 426 5788, ⒲ www.barbados-rentals.com. Pleasant guesthouse a stone's throw from the beach with rooms starting as low as US$30/28 in winter/summer, as well as a communal kitchen, breakfast room, living room and spacious veranda. Comfortable studios that sleep three have recently been added for those wanting private bathrooms and kitchens (US$55/45 in winter/summer). The knowledgeable owner does her best to find budget travellers a cheap room, either at one of her properties or elsewhere.

Bougainvillea Beach Resort

Maxwell ☏ 418 0990, ℻ 428 2524, ⒲ www.bougainvillearesort.com. Popular with British tour groups, this 138-room hotel sits on a lovely stretch of beach and has helpful staff and free water sports to go with its several

▼ CRYSTAL WATERS GUESTHOUSE

pools, tennis courts and evening entertainment. All of the rooms are suites with kitchens (from US$225/149 in winter/summer) and the on-site restaurant (see p.77) is perfectly satisfactory.

Crystal Waters Guesthouse

Worthing ☏ 435 7514. One of the better local guesthouses, with hardwood floors, a TV lounge, a delightful veranda and a laid-back beachside bar nearby (see p.78). Rooms with fan and bathroom from US$37 year round, including breakfast.

Dover Beach Hotel

Dover ☏ 428 8076, ℻ 428 2122, ⒲ www.doverbeach.com. Comfortable, easy-going place located beside a superb beach. The rooms (from US$120/88 in winter/summer) are a bit on the bland side, but they all have a/c and some have kitchenettes. There's also a good-size pool. Ask for a room with a beach or pool view; they're a little more expensive, but worth it.

Little Arches

Miami Beach ☏ 420 4689, ℻ 435 6483, ⒲ www.littlearches.com. Smart boutique hotel a short walk from delightful Miami Beach. The stylish rooms are spacious, with luxurious bathrooms and a/c, though the popular restaurant and bar upstairs can make the place a bit noisy in the late evening (on the other hand, guests must be over 16). There's also a tiny rooftop pool and hammocks to lounge in. Rooms from US$275/192 in winter/summer.

Maraval Guesthouse

Worthing ☏ & ℻ 435 7437, ⒲ www.maravalbarbados.com. Funky little place, popular with European backpackers, with six simple double rooms at US$40 year-round. There's a communal kitchen and eating area and you're close to the beach.

Melbourne Inn

4th Avenue, Dover ☎ 420 5475, ℻ 424 6121, ⊛ www.melbourneinn.com. The rooms are a bit on the tatty side, but the quiet location slightly off the main tourist drag and the friendly atmosphere make for a winning combination. There's also an inexpensive on-site restaurant and an outdoor Jacuzzi (which has great views of planes coming in to the airport). Rooms from US$83/72 in winter/summer.

The Pebble

Paradise Village, St Lawrence Gap ☎ & ℻ 426 5788, ℮ heidrun.rice@ gmx.net. This small yellow house opposite the *Southern Palms Beach Club* has four compact rooms with mosquito nets and fans, a living area, kitchen, bathroom and outside patio. Though the German owner rents out rooms individually (US$40/35 in winter/summer), for groups of up to eight, renting the whole house (US$140/120 in winter/ summer) is a great deal.

Pegwell Inn

Welches, just west of Oistins ☎ 428 6150. This tiny guesthouse is the cheapest place to stay in Barbados. The four simple rooms (from US$20/18 in winter/summer) all have fans and private bathrooms and, though the proximity to the main road can make it a little noisy, it's only a five-minute walk to the beach.

Pirate's Inn

Hastings ☎ 426 6273, ℻ 436 0957, ⊛ www.pirates-inn.com. Friendly hotel within easy strolling distance of Accra Beach, but far enough from the action for those wanting peace and quiet. The rooms (US$120/90 in winter/summer) are spacious and come with well-equipped kitchens, while the attractive little pool and bar with a daily happy hour provide a tempting alternative to the beach.

Roman Beach Apartments

Miami Beach ☎ 428 7635. Lush bougainvillea surrounds this little group of simple apartments, all of which have fans and bathrooms, but no TV or a/c. You're right by a secluded beach, and Oistins is only a five-minute walk away. Rooms from US$65/55 in winter/summer.

Sandy Bay Beach Club

Worthing ☎ 435 8000, ℻ 435 8053, ⊛ www.sandybaybeachclub.com. Big, all-inclusive hotel with a curiously landscaped pool, water sports and regular nightly entertainment. The rooms (from US$216/120 per person in winter/summer) are bright and cheerful, although nothing out of the ordinary, but the beach is so good you'll be spending most of your time there, anyway.

Sea Breeze Beach Hotel

Maxwell ☎ 428 2825, ℻ 428 2872, ⊛ www.sea-breeze.com. Large, nicely laid-out property with two swimming pools, a gym and some outdoor Jacuzzis by a lovely beach. The food is good, too, so those on the optional all-inclusive package are invariably well fed and contented. All rooms come with a/c, TV, fridge and either a balcony or patio; studios have kitchenettes. Rooms from US$191/119 in winter/summer.

Silver Sands Resort

Silver Sands ☎ 428 6001, ℻ 428 3758, ⓦ www.silversandsbarbados.com. The only full-blown resort in the area, elegantly furnished with two restaurants, tennis courts, a large swimming pool and over one hundred air-conditioned rooms (from US$145/80 in winter/summer) spread across well-tended grounds.

Turtle Beach Resort

Dover ☎ 428 7131, ℻ 428 6089, ⓦ www.turtlebeachresortbarbados.com. Top-notch all-inclusive resort, with 164 decent-sized rooms, three restaurants, good water-sports facilities and a kid's club that will keep the young ones entertained all day long. The lovely white-sand beach can get a bit crowded with the hotel's guests, but it's only a short walk to find a quieter patch of sand. All-inclusive rates for two from US$664/434 in winter/summer.

Restaurants

Bay Garden

Oistins Market, Oistins. Daily 5.30–10pm. One of the most distinctive places on the island, "Bay Garden" is really the collective name for the stalls towards the back of the market next to the beach. Each stall has its own name, but they all dish up several kinds of seafood, from spicy conch fritters to fried kingfish and dolphin, as well as tasty side dishes. *Eric's Grill & Bar-Bq* and *Dora's & Jazzie's* next door are particularly good; the former sometimes has lobster. Prices are low: you'll be hard-pressed to pay more than B$20 a head. The covered *Fish Net* stall is a bit more expensive and always very busy, which can mean that your meal may arrive on the slightly cool side.

Bean & Bagel

Dover ☎ 420 4604. Daily 7am–4.30pm. Great coffee, all-day breakfasts, tasty lunch options (sandwiches, salads, pastas and the like) and an Internet café (daily 8am–8pm) have made this a favourite among those staying at the eastern end of St Lawrence Gap. Most meals cost around B$20.

Café Luna

Little Arches, Miami Beach ☎ 420 4689. Daily 8am–9pm. Excellent food served on a terrace at the top of the *Little Arches* hotel (though it's uncovered, so don't go if there's rain in the forecast). Starters include baby octopus and tuna tartare for around B$24–28, while original seafood entrees, such as barracuda, mussels and scallops, make for a refreshing change from the ubiquitous flying fish and dolphin. Most main dishes cost B$65–75.

Captain's Carvery

The Ship Inn, St Lawrence Gap ☎ 420 7447. Daily noon–3pm & 6.30–10.30pm. The restaurant in this huge, nautically themed pub has reasonable Bajan buffet lunches, but most people come for the "Carvery Table" in the evenings, when B$55 buys you unlimited cuts of all meats (beef, ham, lamb, pork and turkey), and plenty of side dishes.

▼ BAY GARDEN

Champers

Rockley, at the east end of Accra Beach ☎434 3463. Mon–Sat 11.30am–3pm & 6–9.45pm. This restaurant has an attractive cliff-top setting and a friendly staff. The kitchen serves up tasty meat and seafood main courses such as blackened chicken with pumpkin risotto and marlin meunière with breadfruit mash and fried okra for B$45–85; there's also an excellent selection of wines.

David's Place

Worthing Main Road (Highway 7), next to the entrance to St Lawrence Gap ☎435 9755. Tues–Sun 6–10pm. The location of *David's Place*, overlooking Little Bay, is striking. The food, however – mostly local dishes like pepperpot stew and curried chicken – is rather average and served in disappointingly small portions. Vegetarians will find more choices than most other places, such as vegetable crepes and lemon-tossed linguine. Main dishes from B$45.

Guang Dong

Worthing Main Road (Highway 7), east end of Worthing ☎435 7387. Daily 11am–3pm & 5.30–10pm. Reliable Chinese restaurant offering typical dishes of sweet-and-sour pork, chow mein and chop suey, from B$15, with particularly good lunchtime combo deals for B$15–28.

Josef's

St Lawrence Gap ☎420 7638. Daily 6.30–10pm. Both the Caribbean-Asian fusion cuisine and the service at this elegant restaurant are as good as you'll find anywhere on the island, with candlelit tables both indoors and, more romantically, down by the water's edge. Starters (B$14–34) include fantastic shredded duck in pancakes with a coconut-and-red curry sauce, while seared yellowfin tuna in a mango sauce and herb-crusted rack of lamb are among the superb main courses (B$58–74).

Just Stop

2nd Avenue, Dover ☎420 8210. Mon–Sat 10am–9pm. Low-key, informal place serving decent, inexpensive local food from a changing daily menu – anything from steakfish, flying fish and curried chicken to a burger and fries – for B$16–25.

Lanterns by the Sea

Bougainvillea Beach Resort, Maxwell ☎418 0990. Daily noon–3pm and 6.30–9.30pm. The best place to eat in Maxwell, with good local and international food including seafood specials (main dishes B$32–50), a barbecue on Mondays and an excellent Caribbean buffet on Thursdays (with accompanying Bajan folk dancing). The atmosphere is relaxed and the views over the water make it a good spot for lunch or early evening.

Pisces

St Lawrence Gap ☎435 6564. Daily 6–10pm. Cavernous but attractive waterside restaurant with a strong emphasis on seafood. Try

▼ PISCES

PLACES The south coast

the calamari (B$24) and octopus ($B23) starters, and the seafood platter of shrimps, scallops, clams and fish (B$66). Service can be spotty, particularly when there's a tour group in, but on the other hand, even when the restaurant is quite full, the sheer size of the place ensures a good chance of getting a table overlooking the water.

Restaurant at Southsea

St Lawrence Gap ☎ 420 7423. Mon–Sat 6–10pm. One of the island's finest dining establishments, thanks to its winning combination of excellent service, romantic setting overlooking a tiny secluded beach and original menu, with starters like ostrich carpaccio and alligator bites (B$30–35), and main dishes of roasted poussin and veal tenderloin (B$60–80).

Sweet Potatoes

St Lawrence Gap ☎ 428 7153. Daily 11.30am–3pm & 6.30–10pm. A lively place with colourful decking and a long wooden bar, *Sweet Potatoes* lives up to its claim of offering "good old Bajan cooking", dishing up tasty starters of fish cakes, marinated codfish and pumpkin-and-spinach fritters (B$13–25) and main courses of jerk pork, mango chicken and stuffed flying fish (B$30–48), all served with a choice of side dishes.

Bars

Bubba's Sports Bar

Rockley, across from the *Accra Beach Hotel* ☎ 435 6217. Mon–Thurs 11.30am–midnight, Fri & Sat 11.30am–1am, Sun 8am–midnight. Matches from around the world are shown on a vast array of big and small screens at this popular sports bar. The food (burgers,

chicken, steaks and sandwiches), while secondary to the night's big games, is decent and reasonably priced, with main courses starting around B$20.

Café Sol

St Lawrence Gap ☎ 435 9531. Daily 6–11pm. Lively, crowded Mexican place that does a roaring trade in margaritas and other tequila-based cocktails (including one with beer!), particularly during the 5–7pm and 10–11pm happy hours. The food – solid Mexican fare (B$25–36) – is sometimes overlooked amid the party atmosphere.

Carib Beach Bar

Worthing, next to *Crystal Waters Guesthouse* ☎ 435 8540. Daily 11am–10pm. While this bar is good for a drink and a snack any night of the week (especially during the Mon–Sat 5–7pm happy hour), it becomes the place to go on Sunday evenings, when locals and tourists alike pack in for a beachside "lime".

Kathy's Bar

Oistins. No phone. Daily 5–11pm. This typical Bajan rum shop in the centre of Oistins Market is a pleasant place to grab a drink and meet some of the locals before heading to the stalls in the *Bay Garden* for a fish dinner (see p.76).

▲ CAFÉ SOL

McBride's Pub

St Lawrence Gap ☎ 435 6352.
Daily 6pm–3am. The inevitable
Irish pub – yes, they do serve
Guinness – *McBride's* is usually
crowded with twenty-something
holiday-makers humming along
to the latest Britpop. Wednesday
nights, with their live reggae
performances, are the most
popular. Bangers and mash go
for B$26, Irish stew for B$28.

Pravda

St Lawrence Gap ☎ 427 1557. Tues–
Sun 6.30pm–3am. Ultra-trendy
(and slightly pretentious) lounges
are relatively new concepts in
Barbados, but this place does its
best to imitate the style with its
all-white decor, intimate lighting
and well-heeled clientele. Asian-
influenced food is also served
(B$48–68).

Whistling Frog Sports Pub

Dover, next to *Time Out at the Gap
Hotel* ☎ 420 5021. Daily 7am–
10.30pm. Most patrons come
to this slightly faded bar-bistro
to hang out with a drink and
watch sports on the TVs. They
also serve food all day – there's a
buffet breakfast, as well as lunch
and supper of shepherd's pie,
pepperpot stew or chicken stir-
fry (all B$20–25). Happy hours
6–7pm and 9–10pm.

Nightlife

Bajan Roots and Rhythms

Plantation Theatre, St Lawrence Gap
☎ 428 5048. Wed & Fri 7pm. B$155
(B$90 for show only). Polished and
popular (albeit very tourist-
oriented) show that relates,
through storytelling and
traditional music and dance,
the history of the island since
the British first landed here.
The B$155 entry fee includes a
Bajan buffet dinner, drinks and
transport to the theatre.

Club Xtreme

Worthing Main Road (Highway 7)
☎ 228 2582. Tues & Sat 10pm–late,
with occasional special events Sun.
The island's only full-fledged
nightclub, complete with a
superb sound system banging
out the latest in dance music,
as well as a big games area with
pool tables and numerous arcade
games. The crowd tends to
be young and, since the cover
charge (B$25–40) includes as
much alcohol as you can drink,
quite flirtatious.

Oistins Market

Oistins. Fri 7pm–1am. If the bars and
clubs in St Lawrence Gap seem
a little empty on Friday nights,
it's because all the locals are at
Oistins Market, the location for
the island's biggest "lime". The
young head to the front part of
the market by the road to dance
to high-tempo Trinidadian soca
and other energetic Caribbean
sounds, while older party-
goers congregate around a bar
called *Lexies* in the back of
the market by the beach for
some more-tranquil ballroom
dancing. Wherever you choose
to be, there is always a great
atmosphere, as well as plenty of
opportunities to meet Bajans.

The Ship Inn

St Lawrence Gap ☎ 420 7447. Daily
10.30pm–3am. English pub in
style, featuring several bars, a
small indoor dance floor, space
to mingle outside and tourist-
friendly bands – think reggae
meets rap meets Marvin Gaye.
There's music most nights from
around 10.30pm–12.30am and an
especially big crowd on Thursdays
when a live band shares centre
stage with several DJs.

The southeast coast

Tourist development has never really taken hold in the southeast of the island. The coastline here is much more rugged than further west, with only a handful of white-sand beaches – several of them, especially Crane Beach and Bottom Bay, quite spectacular – divided from each other by long cliffs and rocky outcrops. The sea is much rougher, too, with Atlantic waves crashing in all year round. Bear this in mind if you are thinking of staying here; while there are several places where you can swim safely, the pounding surf can quickly become overwhelming. If you're not staying, a few attractions in the area are still worth a visit, including an interesting rum factory and an old plantation house. Not surprisingly, nightlife here is nonexistent.

Foul Bay

Three or four kilometres east of the airport, Foul Bay is the largest beach on this section of the coast. Access is signposted: go past the large Methodist Church beside the road in the small village of Rices, then turn right after about 100m – the road will take you right down to the beach. It's a long, wide stretch of white sand; a handful of fishing boats are normally pulled up on the eastern side, and you'll find few tourists (and no food and drink facilities). The long cliffs give the place a rugged feel, though it's not particularly pretty – if you're after a more picturesque "dream" beach, you may want to head for Bottom Bay, a little further northeast.

▲ FOUL BAY

Getting there and around

If you're relying on public transport, **buses** run along the south coast road as far as Sam Lord's Castle, passing the Crane Beach Hotel, though they don't go to any of the beaches – you'll need to walk to them from the main road (usually around 500m). In theory, there are buses that will drop you close to all of the sights mentioned in this chapter, although services are particularly infrequent in the middle of the day; therefore, it's preferable to have your own transport when exploring this part of the island.

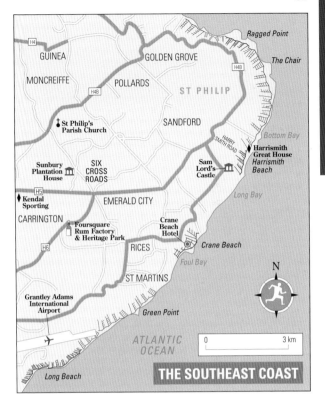

Crane Beach

To the right of the main road, the *Crane Beach Hotel* lies half a kilometre northeast of Foul Bay. Built in 1887, this was one of the first hotels on the island, and it commands a superb site above Crane Bay. In spite of the new timeshare developments behind the hotel (some are already open, others are still under construction), it's a fetching place and worth a look even if you're not staying (a fee of B$25, payable at the hotel reception desk, is charged for use of the facilities, though you can put it towards any food or drink you have during your visit). A long, Roman-style swimming pool runs alongside the main hotel building at the top of the cliff. Beside the restaurant, which offers panoramic views of the coast, two hundred steps lead down to the very pretty Crane Beach (access to the beach via the hotel is included in the B$25 fee; note, however, that steps at the opposite end of the beach are free). Various writers have waxed lyrical about this beach during the last century, but hurricane damage has altered its shape and it is no longer quite as fabulous as they once claimed. On the other side of the pool, another walkway carved into the rock also winds down to the

▲ CRANE BEACH

ocean – this was first cut during the 1760s to provide a discreet bathing spot for women, but is no longer in use.

Sam Lord's Castle

Long Bay. Five minutes' drive northeast of Crane Bay, Sam Lord's Castle was built in 1820 by Sam Lord, a legendary local crook who reputedly made his fortune by luring ships onto a nearby reef and salvaging anything of value from the resultant wrecks. Though local historians question the veracity of this story, there is no doubt that Lord made enough money from one dubious source or another to employ craftsmen from England to build parts of his mansion in the style of Windsor Castle. Unfortunately, the property and its grounds are currently closed to the public, although a Trinidadian company has recently

---

Bussa's rebellion

In 1807 the British government banned the transfer of slaves from Africa to the Caribbean. While the measure had little immediate impact on Barbadian planters, who preferred Creole slaves born on the island, it did add fuel to the growing movement for the overall abolition of slavery. In an attempt to deflect criticism, Barbadian planters made some token improvements to the slaves' conditions: women's working hours were reduced, whites could be punished for murdering blacks and slaves were permitted to own property.

The slaves, though, knew that none of these concessions had been made willingly, and rumours spread claiming that emancipation had been proclaimed in Britain but was being blocked on the island. The situation reached its boiling point in April 1816, when Barbados faced its only serious slave uprising. **Bussa's Rebellion** – named after its leader, an African-born slave who was head ranger at a plantation in St Philip – began in the southeast with attacks on property and fires in sugar fields. It quickly spread throughout the southern and central parishes, and the slaves fought several pitched battles against white militias and British troops. They never stood a chance: within three days the rebellion was crushed, with only a handful of white casualties but over a thousand slaves either killed in battle (including Bussa himself) or executed afterwards, along with prominent free coloured supporters of emancipation. There were no further outbreaks of major violence, but the abolitionist movement in Britain continued to gather momentum until slavery was finally outlawed in 1834.

Harrismith and Bottom Bay practicalities

To get to **Harrismith**, stay on the main road as it veers left past the turn-off to Sam Lord's Castle and follow it until you arrive at the intersection with Highway 5. Turn right on Highway 5 and after about 500m, turn right again on "Harry Smith Road". Follow the road another 500m or so, then turn left onto a rutted track. At the bottom of the track is the deserted Harrismith Great House (see below). The blue, government buses to Sam Lord's Castle turn around to go back to Bridgetown 100m before the Harry Smith Road turn-off, from which it's a twenty-minute walk to the beach.

To reach **Bottom Bay**, continue along Highway 5 past Harry Smith Road for a minute or so – the turning is signposted on the right. Park at the top of the cliffs and walk down the steps.

purchased Sam Lord's Castle with plans to refurbish and re-open it as a luxury hotel. At the time of writing, opening dates had yet to be announced.

Harrismith and Bottom Bay

Beyond Sam Lord's Castle are a couple of good beaches worth checking out. The first, Harrismith Beach, is overshadowed by the old, abandoned **Harrismith Great House**, a former hotel overlooking Harrismith Beach. There is nothing to stop you poking around inside the house, although be careful of loose debris and uneven surfaces. Just west of the house, steps lead down to the pretty and usually very quiet beach, which is strewn with palms, cliffs and small caves ideal for exploring. Bottom Bay, the next stretch north from Harrismith, is even nicer: the small sugar-white beach is sandwiched between cliffs and framed by palm trees and crashing Atlantic waves. Few visitors make the effort to find the place (see box, above), although locals use it at the weekend and the occasional tour bus heads this way during the week.

The Foursquare Rum Factory and Heritage Park

Just southwest of Six Cross Roads ☎420 9954 or 420 1977 for tours.

▼ HARRISMITH

Mon–Fri 9am–4pm. Free; B$25 for the optional tour. Back on Highway 5, if you head west, you'll come to the Foursquare Rum Factory and Heritage Park, near Six Cross Roads. The ultra-modern distillery sits on the site of an ancient sugar estate, smack in the middle of sweeping fields of sugar cane. The Foursquare sugar plantation was established in the 1640s during the earliest days of sugar in Barbados, and the present-day factory combines state-of-the-art design with traditional features and buildings. You are free to wander around on your own and view the gleaming factory with its modern boilers and fermentation tanks. Private tours, meanwhile, must be booked 48 hours in advance and are only worthwhile if you want an explanation of how the rum is actually produced – and a free drink at the end of the tour.

The factory's 250-year-old foundry, a long, elegant building of thick coral stone blocks, now serves as a trendy art gallery for paintings and sculptures by Bajan artists and occasional exhibitions of work from around the Caribbean. Most of the pieces are for sale, and you can also buy bottles of the ESA Field rum made in the factory. Dotted around the site

are craft studios that make and sell wicker baskets, leather bags and jewellery, as well as stalls offering snacks and drinks.

Sunbury Plantation House

Just northwest of Six Cross Roads ☏ 423 6270. Daily 10am–5pm. B$15. A short drive north of the Foursquare Rum Factory, Sunbury is one of the oldest and – for the sheer variety of furniture, artwork and colonial-era bits and pieces – most interesting of the island's great houses. The entry fee includes a guided tour of the interior, after which you're free to wander through the main rooms and around the extensive gardens, or have a snack at the small outdoor café.

Ownership of the sugar estate dates back to the very first settlers in Barbados, although the house itself dates from the mid-eighteenth century. From 1835 to 1981, the plantation was owned by the family of local shipping merchant Thomas Daniel, a friend of the notorious Sam Lord (see p.82). Gutted by fire in 1995, the building has been restored to look almost exactly as it did beforehand. Although only the walls are original, built with local coral blocks and ballast from British ships and made 50cm thick to withstand hurricane winds, the restoration has brilliantly recaptured the period feel of the rooms, helped by donations of furniture and other artefacts from around the island. There is a wealth of old mahogany pieces on the ground floor – the massive claw-footed dining table is beautiful – while the walls are lined with prints and paintings of old Barbados. Upstairs, the bedrooms show off nineteenth- and early

▼ SUNBURY PLANTATION HOUSE

▲ L'AZURE RESTAURANT

twentieth-century fashions, including Victorian underwear and suit-like 1920s swimming costumes; back downstairs, the cellars are stuffed with paraphernalia from traditional plantation life, including horse-drawn buggies, cooking pots, cutlery and the sad, charred relics of the 1995 fire.

Accommodation

Crane Beach Hotel

☎ 423 6220, 🖷 423 5343, 🖲 www.thecrane.com. With a stunning setting high above Crane Bay, this once small and exclusive hotel has been thoroughly changed by the on-going addition of adjoining timeshare apartment blocks. Noise from the construction is not overly intrusive, however, and the place remains luxurious, with rooms (some with their own plunge pools) decked out in mahogany furniture and two excellent restaurants. The superb beach is reached via a long staircase (see p.81). Rooms from US$347/165 in winter/summer.

Restaurants

L'Azure

Crane Beach Hotel ☎ 423 6220. Daily noon–3pm & 6.30–9.30pm. Overlooking the bay and serving excellent, albeit slightly unimaginative, seafood dishes like seared mahi mahi and grilled swordfish (B$30–40 at lunch, B$40–60 at dinner), this is the main restaurant of the *Crane Beach Hotel*. It makes a good lunch stop if you're in the area, but bear in mind that the place can lack atmosphere out of season. Sundays see a buffet breakfast (B$40) and lunch (B$70), the former accompanied by a gospel choir, the latter by steel pan music.

Zen

Crane Beach Hotel ☎ 423 6220. Daily 6–9pm. Classy and elegant, serving Japanese- and Thai-accented dishes. The delicious but pricey sushi, sashimi and tempura are all good choices, while zesty red, green and yellow curries (all B$36) add some spice. A large glass wall provides dramatic ocean views.

The west coast

The sandy beaches and warm Caribbean waters of Barbados's sheltered west coast – the so-called platinum coast – have made it the island's prime resort area. Much of the coastline has been heavily developed, and is now home to the island's top restaurants, priciest hotels and most sought-after private homes. There is, however, still a smattering of reasonably priced places to stay, and all of the beaches have free public access. Should you tire of lounging in the sun, the area has other attractions as well, including lively, modern Holetown, with its fine old church and legion of shopping opportunities, and Speightstown, where colonial relics and picturesque old streets recall its vanished heyday as a major port.

Paynes Bay and around

There is little sign of the tourist extravaganza to come as Highway 1 clears Bridgetown and begins carving its way up the west coast through the tiny village of Prospect. Most of the buildings here are residential, and the beaches – largely devoid of tourists, except for the stretches backed by the area's few hotels – are really only full on weekends and holidays, when families living near the capital come to take the air.

Coming from Bridgetown, the first of these beaches, **Batts Rock Park**, is a large, slightly scruffy zone with a couple of lifeguard towers and a picnic area. A better bet if you want to swim is **Prospect Beach**, a little further north up the coast. A narrow crescent of sand, it leads onto a calm turquoise bay. Public access is via a path just north of the *Escape Hotel*; at times the beach can get crowded with the hotel's guests.

Most visitors, though, keep heading north to Paynes Bay, one of the most popular beaches on the west coast. Some good restaurants and a smattering

Getting there and around

It could hardly be easier to get around on the west coast. North of Bridgetown, Highway 1 runs up the coast, rarely straying more than 100m from the shoreline. The larger and more direct Highway 2A runs parallel to it a little way inland, and offers a speedier way of getting to the north of the island. **Buses** and **minibuses** ply the coast road between Bridgetown and Speightstown all day, and there are bus stops every few hundred metres. Services normally stop at around midnight, after which time you'll need a car or private **taxi**. If you're coming from Bridgetown, catch a minibus at the Princess Alice Bus Station in Cheapside; visitors coming from the south coast should look for buses marked "Speightstown" – these usually bypass Bridgetown and save you having to change buses (and terminals) in the city.

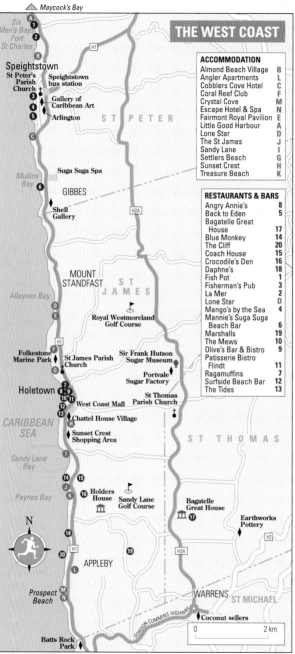

△ Maycock's Bay

THE WEST COAST

Six
Men's Bay
Port
St Charles

Speightstown
St Peter's
Parish
Church

Speightstown
bus station

Gallery of
Caribbean Art

Arlington

ST PETER

ACCOMMODATION

Almond Beach Village	B
Angler Apartments	L
Cobblers Cove Hotel	C
Coral Reef Club	F
Crystal Cove	M
Escape Hotel & Spa	N
Fairmont Royal Pavilion	E
Little Good Harbour	A
Lone Star	D
The St James	J
Sandy Lane	I
Settlers Beach	G
Sunset Crest	H
Treasure Beach	K

Mullins
Bay

Suga Suga Spa

GIBBES

Shell
Gallery

RESTAURANTS & BARS

Angry Annie's	8
Back to Eden	5
Bagatelle Great House	17
Blue Monkey	14
The Cliff	20
Coach House	15
Crocodile's Den	16
Daphne's	18
Fish Pot	1
Fisherman's Pub	3
La Mer	2
Lone Star	D
Mango's by the Sea	4
Mannie's Suga Suga Beach Bar	6
Marshalls	19
The Mews	10
Olive's Bar & Bistro	9
Patisserie Bistro Flindt	11
Ragamuffins	7
Surfside Beach Bar	12
The Tides	13

MOUNT
STANDFAST

ST
JAMES

Alleynes Bay

Royal Westmoreland
Golf Course

Folkestone
Marine Park

St James Parish
Church

Sir Frank Hutson
Sugar Museum

Portvale
Sugar Factory

Holetown

West Coast Mall

Chattel House Village

St Thomas
Parish Church

CARIBBEAN
SEA

Sunset Crest
Shopping Area

ST THOMAS

Sandy Lane
Bay

Paynes Bay

Holders
House

Sandy Lane
Golf Course

Bagatelle
Great House

Earthworks
Pottery

N

APPLEBY

Prospect
Beach

WARRENS   ST MICHAEL

GORDON CUMMINS HIGHWAY

◆ Coconut sellers

Batts Rock
Park

0   2 km

of nightlife options line this attractive stretch of white sand, but the atmosphere is normally laid-back and family-oriented. The only exception to this rule is when a cruise ship docks at Bridgetown's Deep Water Harbour and passengers are bussed to the northern end of the beach for a day's sunbathing. At other times, catamarans and other pleasure-craft drop anchor 50m offshore, opposite *The St James*, so that tourists can swim with the handful of turtles that show up here to be fed.

Holders House

Holders Hill, just inland from Paynes Bay. Closed to the public for most of the year, every March this gorgeous old plantation house and private home hosts the Caribbean's leading festival of classical music, Holders Season. Though it may seem somewhat incongruous to hear operas and classical concerts performed by singers and musicians in period costume outdoors under mahogany and palm trees, the spectacular setting invests the whole thing with a magical air. Little expense is spared: quality performers are flown in specially from Britain, and the organisers generally put together an imaginative schedule. Recent seasons have included a restaging of *Inkle and Yarico* – an eighteenth-century opera based on a traditional Barbadian legend that was once all the rage in London's West End – as well as a concert by Pavarotti and, away from the classical sphere, a celebration of calypso music with contributions by top performers from Trinidad and Barbados. For details, see the festival website (ⓦ www.holders .net), or contact the Barbados

Tourism Authority (☎ 427 2623, Ⓕ 426 4080) or Holders House direct (☎ 432 6385, Ⓕ 432 6461).

During the winter, the immaculate grounds are open for **polo** matches, usually on alternate Saturday afternoons. For match schedules, call the Barbados Polo Club (☎ 432 1802).

Bagatelle Great House

Bagatelle ☎ 421 6767. Mon–Fri noon–2.30pm & 6.30–10pm, Sat 6.30–10pm. Follow Holders Hill east until it intersects with Highway 2A at the Shell service station. A few hundred metres north of here lies Bagatelle Great House, one of the best examples of early Barbadian vernacular architecture. According to legend, the great house was given its name by a former owner who, having lost the estate in a dice game, derided it as "a mere bagatelle".

The house is now home to an upscale restaurant (see p.98), but the rest of the building is still open to the public during the restaurant's hours of operation. Inside, a classic double staircase leads up to the old living quarters (where there are occasional displays of local art; ask someone in the restaurant to let you in if the door is locked), which are fronted by a columned porch with a decorated pediment. The doors below the porch lead into deep cellars that once served as the house's food-storage area and are now the restaurant's dining room and wine bar.

Earthworks Pottery

2 Edgehill Heights ☎ 425 0223, ⓦ www.earthworks-pottery.com. Mon–Fri 9am–5pm, Sat 9am–1pm. The factory and shops here are worth a short detour off the

▲ SANDY LANE

main highway – from Bagatelle Great House head back south on Highway 2A past the Shell service station until you reach a shop called Automotive Arts; turn left here and follow the signs. (If you're feeling thirsty, continue south until you reach the roundabout at Warrens, where you'll find people selling bottles of fresh **coconut water** by the roadside for about B\$9.) Organized in 1975 to support the island's declining pottery industry (based largely at Chalky Mount; see p.107), Earthworks and its products have developed a great following among both Bajans and tourists alike. This is a good place to come for colourful souvenirs: there are racks of mugs, jugs, plates and vases for sale, and you can watch the potters at work.

Sandy Lane

Sandy Lane Bay. Back on the coast, just north of Paynes Bay, the *Sandy Lane Hotel* is by far the island's grandest accommodation – the epitome of Caribbean affluence and ostentation, it has a list of repeat celebrity guests as long as your arm (see p.97). Built in the early 1960s by Anglo–American Ronald Tree, a former parliamentary adviser to the government of Sir Winston Churchill, the hotel was designed to provide a winter retreat for the British upper class. These days, the likes of Mick Jagger and Michael Caine are regular visitors, and the place guards its guests jealously behind high walls and security guards.

Despite all the security, as part of his deal with the government to get permission for the hotel (and the re-routing of the coastal road that it involved), Tree had to provide a ten-metre right-of-way for public access to the shore – it's along the southern edge of the property. Take advantage of this loophole, and wander down to the bay, past the tall casuarina and manchineel trees. The stretch of sand, backed by the elegant hotel (completely rebuilt between 1998 and 2001), is quite magnificent.

The hotel's golf course, which sits between Highway 1 and Highway 2A, is also open to the public. For details, see p.140.

Holetown

It was in present-day Holetown, a five-minute drive north of Sandy Lane, that English sailors first landed in Barbados in 1625, claiming the island for their king, James I, and naming the area St James' Town. Two years later, a vessel named

▲ HOLETOWN RIVER

William and John landed at the same spot, carrying a party of settlers; they renamed the place Holetown – the inlet where they had anchored their ship reminded them of the Hole on the River Thames in London. The place developed slowly, eventually losing favour to the site of present-day Bridgetown, whose natural harbours offered better protection for shipping. Today, Holetown has become a busy, local hub for the tourist industry, though it does somewhat lack in character. All west coast buses run through the town, and the main highway is lined with fast-food restaurants, souvenir shops, banks and grocery stores.

Sunset Crest, Chattel House Village and the West Coast Mall

As you approach Holetown from the south, Sunset Crest will appear on the east side of the highway. The small shopping centre has a few ordinary souvenir shops selling T-shirts, books and liquor, and if you're there on Sundays, vendors hawking fresh coconut water by the roadside (on other days, head to Warrens to buy coconut water – see p.89). There are additional shopping options in Holetown itself: a dozen reproduction chattel houses

next to the highway sell more interesting gifts and souvenirs, and there are jewellery stores and clothes shops, as well as a supermarket, at the nearby West Coast Mall.

James Fort and the Hole

Holetown. West of Highway 1 – which runs through Holetown – there are a couple of small roads where you can cut down to the beach; it's less than 100m from the main drag. However, the sand is often crowded and narrow and you're better off heading out of town if you want to swim. Also west of the highway, in the centre of Holetown, the pale blue police station is built on the site of the old James Fort, a few of whose iron cannons still sit outside. Next to the cannons is an obelisk, known as the Holetown Monument, which was erected in 1905 to commemorate the 300th anniversary of the arrival of the first settlers. Historians turned out to be several decades off with their calculations, but this didn't stop anyone from enjoying a huge celebratory street party. An unapologetic corrective plaque was quietly fixed to the bottom of the obelisk in 1977 to mark the 350th anniversary of the first settlement.

A minute's walk north of here, 1st and 2nd Streets, lined with

▲ JAMES FORT

The story of sugar

Commercial **sugar** production began in Barbados in 1643, when Dutch traders introduced sugar cane plants from Brazil, heralding a dramatic change in the island's fortunes. The original dense forest that covered Barbados was chopped down to leave bare land suitable for the new plantations, and the frontier farming communities of European migrants were replaced by a slave-based plantation society as Africans were brought in to labour in the sugar fields.

Barbados was England's first sugar-producing colony, and it provided fabulous returns for plantation owners for well over a century. The island gradually began to lose ground to nearby Jamaica, but tax and trade incentives meant that growing sugar remained lucrative, and the planters celebrated their wealth by building the lavish great houses that still overlook cane fields from breezy hilltops. However, the industry took two big hits in the mid-nineteenth century when the abolition of the slave trade in 1834 was followed by the British Sugar Equalization Act of 1846, which ended preferential treatment for sugar produced in the colonies.

Though no longer able to compete effectively with cheaper sugar from Cuba and Brazil, the Barbadian sugar industry has rumbled on into the 21st century. In recent decades, attempts to save the industry have included the centralization of factories and the introduction of modern machinery. The windmills are no longer turning, but swaying fields of cane still dominate the island, testament to the continuing importance of King Sugar.

trendy restaurants, lead down to the sea. Further on, the scenery becomes more bucolic, with fields, cows and a cricket pitch by the side of the road; a bridge runs over the Hole itself, which is alive with egrets towards sunset.

St James Parish Church

Holetown. Daily 9am–5pm. Free. St James Parish Church is one of the most attractive parish churches on the island, and also the oldest religious site in Barbados – the first wooden church was constructed here in 1628. This original building was replaced by a stone structure in 1660 but, as happened throughout the island, hurricane and fire damage took their toll, and most of the present building, including the elegant round tower above the altar, dates from between 1789 and 1874, when the nave was extended. However, there are older relics: the stone pillars at the entrance to the south porch

are thought to be from the seventeenth century, while the baptismal font and the iron bell in the north porch are dated 1684 and 1696, respectively.

The present church is a small but graceful building, with thick stone walls, and a stone chancel arch that divides the nave from the choir. There are the usual marble funerary monuments on the walls, as well as more modern works of art, including a colourful biblical triptych by Ethiopian painter Alemayehu Bizuneh and bronze bas-reliefs of St James and St Mary by Czech sculptor George Kveton. There are also extracts from the church's old parish register, which recorded the short lives of the early settlers, and a letter from the White House expressing Ronald and Nancy Reagan's appreciation of a service they attended here in 1982. Reagan's currying of favour with Caribbean leaders paid off a year later when the majority – headed by Barbados's Tom Adams – gave avid support to the US invasion of Grenada.

Folkestone Marine Park

Entrance just north of Holetown. Mon–Fri 9am–5pm. Free beach access; B$1.15 for visitor centre. Established in 1979, the Folkestone Marine Park extends down the coast as far as Sandy Lane Bay. For **snorkellers** there are some decent patches of coral reef just offshore; alternatively, you can usually find a glass-bottomed boat to take you out to hunt for colourful fish and the occasional turtle. The visitor centre has a short video and a handful of reasonable displays on the island's coral reefs and other aspects of marine life. If you're just into loafing around, the beach outside the centre – a decent if very narrow and rather rocky stretch – is popular with local families on weekends and holidays, and has a lifeguard, showers, snack bars and a sprinkling of beach vendors.

Sir Frank Hutson Sugar Museum and Portvale Sugar Factory

Just west of Highway 2A ☎ 426 2421. Mon–Sat 8am–5pm. B$25 including factory tour, B$10 museum only. Just to the north of the West Coast Mall in the centre of Holetown, a road leads east to join Highway 2A. Turn left when you reach the highway, and a few hundred metres up on the left you'll see the Portvale Sugar Factory. Next to the factory is the small but informative Sir Frank Hutson Sugar Museum, which offers a clear introduction to the product on which Barbados depended for nearly three hundred years.

Housed in the former boiling house of the Blowers sugar estate, which was built in the 1880s, the museum showcases a series of "tayches". These large boiling pans were used to heat the cane juice; the scum or waste floated to the top and was ladled off before the residue was passed into the next, smaller pan en route to being turned into crystals. Elsewhere, there are giant pieces of mill machinery, as well as the tools of the blacksmiths and coopers who helped keep the estate running smoothly. However, it is the museum's old black-and-white photos that best evoke the era in which sugar was king. The pictures show workers slaving in the fields, grinding the cane and racing the barrels of sugar through the streets of Bridgetown to catch the next boat to England.

Between February and June (the reaping season), the museum's entrance price also includes a tour of the factory (at other times, you can only visit the museum) – a heady experience for the smell alone – where you can view the full production process, from the loading and grinding of the cane to the crystallization of the brown sugar, which is sent off for refining abroad. The factory was built in 1984 and, during its relatively short operating season, takes cane from 33 local plantations and more than six hundred small farmers. At the end of the tour you'll be presented with a bag of sugar made at the factory.

North to Mullins Bay

Back on the coast, Highway 1 continues north beyond the Folkestone Marine Park. Mullins Bay – a strip of sugary sand with a lively beach bar (see p.101 for review) – is a good place to pause for a swim. Buses make stops here, and there's a car park across from the bay.

Next to the car park, the **Suga Suga Spa** (☎419 4507; daily 9am–6pm) is ideal for passing a decadent afternoon being pampered and groomed. A complete range of treatments is offered, with something for about every budget; most are B$60–125.

Otherwise, there's not much of particular interest between Folkestone and Speightstown – a series of exclusive hotels and grand private estates, hidden behind security gates, is interspersed with small villages of shops, fishing shacks and chattel houses trying to keep a Bajan toehold in the increasingly developed area.

▲ SPEIGHTSTOWN

Speightstown

Small, run-down and utterly charming, Speightstown (pronounced "Spikestown") is the second largest town in Barbados, though it remains largely untouched by tourist development. Once a thriving port, it was famous for its tough-talking, uncompromising inhabitants – "Speightstown flattery" is an old Bajan term for a backhanded compliment. Over the last century, however, the place has declined precipitately; old buildings were left to decay, and a great fire in 1941 destroyed many of the town's older sites. Recent years have seen serious efforts to preserve and recreate Speightstown's historical character, turning it into a "model town", but it remains an earthy, beguiling place, with old-fashioned Georgian-style shops lining narrow streets, their galleries – propped up on

wooden pillars – projecting over the pavements. There is little to do here but stroll around the remnants of the local fishing industry and a few stylish old buildings or dine at one of a handful of excellent restaurants.

Buses running up the west coast normally terminate at Speightstown, stopping at the eastern end of Church Street – from here, head down towards the sea and you'll pass the parish church on your right. Queen Street has an unofficial tourist information office in the *Fisherman's Pub* (see p.99).

St Peter's Parish Church

Church Street, Speightstown. Daily 9am–5pm. Free. Across from the Speightstown Esplanade, this church was first built in the 1630s, making it one of the oldest churches in Barbados. Destroyed by the 1831 hurricane, the Georgian building was rebuilt in a graceful Greek Revival style – though with the standard tower tacked on for good measure – and the present incarnation was superbly restored after the place was ruined by fire in 1980. It's an airy, peaceful place, as you'd expect, though there's nothing particularly eye-catching.

Queen Street

Speightstown's main drag has several grand old buildings

that have survived the town's decline. Opposite *Mango's by the Sea* restaurant, **Arlington**, almost medieval in design, is a classic example of the island's early townhouses – narrow, tall and gabled, with a sharply sloping roof. The iron gateway and outside veranda were common features among the homes of wealthy Speightstown merchants; this house belonged to a ship's chandler, with its shop downstairs and the family home on the two floors above. The building is currently closed to the public, although it may re-open as a museum and theatre. For the latest news, contact the Barbados National Trust (℡426 2421).

While you're here, cross the road and check out the **Gallery of Caribbean Art** (℡419 0858; Mon–Fri 9.30am–4.30pm, Sat 9.30am–2pm) above the RBC bank. There are three rooms full of paintings, sculptures and metalwork for sale by artists from Barbados and the wider Caribbean.

At the north end of town, a couple of hundred metres past St Peter's Parish Church, the **art gallery** of the self-styled Gang of Four (℡419 0051; Mon–Sat 9am–4pm) makes its home in a fading yellow house with a veranda overlooking the beach. It's worth a look for the local Impressionist- and

▲ FISH MARKET, SIX MEN'S BAY

Expressionist-influenced paintings of Gordon Webster, Lilian Sten and Azziza, and the sculpture of Ras Bongo Congo.

Six Men's Bay

Heading north from Speightstown, the main road passes the spectacular Port St Charles marina, where luxury apartments with their own yachting berths change hands for millions of dollars. Beyond here is a series of small, quiet fishing villages; perhaps the most picturesque of these is the former whaling port of Six Men's Bay, where brightly painted boats line the shore.

Maycock's Bay

The lovely area occupying the extreme northwestern tip of the island contains the site of Maycock's Fort, one of the

▼ MAYCOCK'S BAY

island's principal defences in the seventeenth century. It was built in 1638, just north of a small river inlet, to protect against enemy incursions. Sadly, the fort's ancient coral stone walls and powder magazines are now almost completely ruined, causing few people to make the effort to reach it, even though it's just a short stroll down from the end of the paved track.

Shops

Best of Barbados

Chattel House Village, Holetown ☎432 4691. Mon–Sat 9am–5pm, Sun 9.30am–1pm. Upmarket and relatively tasteful souvenirs, from locally made creams and lotions to prints of island scenes, sold with enthusiasm by the friendly staff. Other locations in Bridgetown, St Lawrence Gap, Hastings, the airport and the seaport.

La Galerie Antique

Paynes Bay ☎432 6094. Mon–Fri 10am–5pm, Sat 10am–1pm. Stuffed with pieces of china, porcelain, silverware and furniture, most of them gleaned from the island's plantation houses, this antiques shop is like a small museum.

Shell Gallery

Gibbes ☎422 2593. Mon–Fri 9am–5pm, Sat 9am–2pm. Just before Mullins Bay, a signposted turn-off to the right leads up to this delightful little shop selling a fantastic collection of shells, both individually or as the main component of pictures, frames and jewellery, among other items. It's worth a look even if you're not planning to buy.

Accommodation

Almond Beach Village

Heywoods ☎422 4900, ⓕ422 0617, ⓦwww.almondresorts.com. This large and popular all-inclusive hotel spreads along a lengthy stretch of beach just north of Speightstown. Besides numerous bars, restaurants and activities, there are eleven pools, a small golf course, a nursery and a kids' club. If, for some reason, you're feeling bored by all this, there are squash and tennis courts, too. All-inclusive rates from US$730/605 for two people in winter/summer.

Angler Apartments

Derricks ☎ & ⓕ432 0817, ⓦwww.barbadosahoy.com/angler. Fourteen adequate, air-conditioned, self-catering apartments in three small blocks. Shaded by mango and breadfruit trees, they're set back 200m from the highway and are just five minutes' walk from a good beach. Rooms from US$135/105 in winter/summer.

Cobblers Cove Hotel

Between Speightstown and Mullins Bay ☎422 2291, ⓕ422 1460, ⓦwww.cobblerscove.com. Forty spacious suites are cleverly hidden around a large, beautiful garden at *Cobblers Cove*. The main building – bright pink in colour but English country house in decor – holds a splendid bar and restaurant (as well as two spectacular suites with canopy beds, Jacuzzis and plunge pools) and opens onto a pleasant and relatively empty beach. Overall, one of the most delightful hotels on the island. Rooms from US$730/480 in winter/summer.

▲ CRYSTAL COVE

Coral Reef Club

St James Beach ☎ 422 2372, ℱ 422 1776, ⓦ www.coralreefbarbados .com. Set in lush, jungle-like gardens and centred round a breezy main building, the accommodation here is in attractive rooms or small cottages. There is no real beach to speak of, although two swimming pools, a lovely open-plan restaurant, tennis courts and complimentary water sports make up for the lack of sand. Rooms from US$420/210 in winter/summer.

Crystal Cove

Appleby ☎ 432 2683, ℱ 432 8290, ⓦ www.crystalcovehotelbarbados .com. One of the island's best all-inclusive hotels, with comfortable rooms, excellent food, good water sports and several pools (one has a swim-up bar under a waterfall). It's one of four west coast hotels owned by Elegant Hotels (all are connected by a free boat taxi), and you're welcome to use the facilities at the sister hotels as well (though you must pay a supplement for dinner at those which aren't all-inclusive). All-inclusive rates for two people

from US$548/364 in winter/summer.

Escape Hotel & Spa

Prospect Bay ☎ & ℱ 424 7571, ⓦ www.escapehotels.co.uk. Unpretentious all-inclusive accommodation operated by Virgin Holidays and decorated in bright, pastel colours. This is the only hotel on a great stretch of beach, and there are plenty of water sports options, including windsurfing, sailing and kayaking. The food is pretty good, too. Ask for an ocean-view room on the second floor, or, if you want to be far from kids, a room in the adult-only spa across the road. All-inclusive rates for two people from US$789/194 in winter/summer.

Fairmont Royal Pavilion

Porters ☎ 422 5555, ℱ 422 3940, ⓦ www.fairmont.com/royalpavilion. Large but peaceful hotel surrounded by verdant gardens. Many of the rooms face the ocean, and all of them come with DVD players and either a balcony or a patio. The beach here is better than at the hotels just to the north and south and there are complimentary water sports and tennis. Rooms from US$739/359 in winter/summer.

Little Good Harbour

Shermans ☎ 439 3000, ℱ 439 2020, ⓦ www.littlegoodharbourbarbados.com. Friendly little hotel in a quiet spot north of Speightstown. Welcoming one- and two-bedroom suites are in wooden gingerbread cottages, complete with kitchens, balconies and four-poster beds. There's also a good restaurant next door.

Rooms from US$335/237 in winter/summer.

Lone Star

Mount Standfast ☎ 419 0599, ℻ 419 0597, 🌐 thelonestar.com. Fabulous, ultra-trendy and highly recommended little boutique hotel with four spectacular suites right on the beach. The massive rooms feature walk-in showers, wooden floors and stylish furniture, and each has a veranda the size of most ordinary hotel rooms. Rooms from US$650/375 in winter/summer.

Mango Lane Apartments

Speightstown ☎ 422 3146 or 422 2703. An assortment of colourful and sparsely furnished chattel houses and apartments dotted around the local area, rented out by the friendly owners of the *Fishermen's Pub* in Speightstown from US$40 per night all year round.

The St James

Paynes Bay ☎ 432 0489, ℻ 432 2824, 🌐 the-stjames.com. Formerly *Beachcomber Suites*, this small apartment block by the beach has been wonderfully refurbished, and now offers some of the largest, most luxurious and well-equipped studios (sleeping two) and two-bedroom apartments (sleeping up to six; great value for groups) on the island. The apartments have modern kitchens and huge balconies overlooking Paynes Bay; the studios come with kitchenettes and smaller balconies. Rooms from US$275/180 in winter/summer.

Sandy Lane

Sandy Lane ☎ 444 2000, ℻ 444 2222, 🌐 sandylane.com. The jewel of the west coast, *Sandy Lane* is a magnificent place in every way,

offering spectacularly luxurious rooms, restaurants, bars, a spa and other communal areas. If you need to ask the price you can't afford it. Rooms from US$1100/850 in winter/summer.

Settlers Beach

Settlers Beach ☎ 422 3052, ℻ 422 1937, 🌐 settlersbeachhotel.com. Delightful hotel on a cosy stretch of beach, attractively landscaped and with a fine freshwater swimming pool. The 22 spacious two-bedroom villas (from US$227/112 in winter/summer) all have kitchens, small libraries and gardens, and sleep up to five people. A good choice for families and groups.

Sunset Crest

Sunset Crest ☎ 432 6750, ℻ 432 7229, 🌐 sunsetcrestbarbados .com. Large, sprawling resort ten minutes' walk from the beach, with several swimming pools, restaurants and bars, and over a hundred one-bedroom apartments and two- and three-bedroom cottages scattered around the complex. Rooms (from US$125/90 in winter/summer) are rather austere and you have to buy tokens to operate the a/c.

Treasure Beach

Paynes Bay ☎ 432 1346, ℻ 432 1094, 🌐 treasurebeachhotel .com. Small, unpretentious and charming boutique hotel, with 35 stylish one-bedroom suites (from US$765/265 in winter/summer) arranged around a pretty little swimming pool. Recently refurbished, the comfortable and well-appointed rooms have a separate living area and either a balcony or patio, while two luxury suites boast plunge pools and terraces overlooking the sea. The hotel

▲ ANGRY ANNIE'S

restaurant is first-rate, there's a fitness centre and the staff is one of the friendliest around.

Restaurants

Angry Annie's

1st Street, Holetown ☎ 432 2119. Daily 6–10pm. Brightly painted building (with equally colourful interior decor), just off the main highway. The menu includes a decent selection of local food – starters of fisherman's soup or flying fish filets for around B$14–20, and main courses of multicoloured Rasta pasta (B$35), chicken curry (B$44) or "limbo lamb" (lamb shank; B$55).

Back to Eden

Jordan's Plaza, Queen Street, Speightstown ☎ 422 0410. Mon–Fri 10am–4pm. One of very few vegetarian establishments in Barbados, this friendly and informal place serves tasty island stews and other health-conscious dishes. The refreshing and unusual juices deserve special mention: depending on the season, you can sample carambola, golden plum and even sea-moss drinks. Lunches for B$7, B$10 or B$12.

Bagatelle Great House

Bagatelle ☎ 421 6767. Mon–Fri noon–2.30pm & 6.30–10pm, Sat 6.30–10pm. The musty cellars of the Great House provide a wonderful setting full of colonial character for this upscale restaurant. The fine, European-influenced cuisine includes such starters as a stilton-and-walnut tart and foie gras (B$20–39) and main courses of roast pheasant and braised belly of pork with mashed potato, apple sauce and crackling (B$42–89). There is also a good selection of wines.

Blue Monkey ~~closed~~

Paynes Bay ☎ 432 7528. Daily noon–9.30pm. An inexpensive and informal alternative to the pricey restaurants in this area, *Blue Monkey* serves an eclectic mix of lasagna, jerked pork schnitzel, lobster burgers and flying fish (B$15–36) beside the beach for lunch and dinner.

The Cliff

Fitts ☎ 432 1922. Dec–April daily 6.30–9pm, May–Nov Mon–Sat 6.30–9pm. A meal at this longstanding west coast favourite, located in a beautiful, coral building on a cliff-top, comes complete with exquisite food with an international (especially Asian) flavour, flaming torches and a small army of (perhaps overly) attentive waiters. On the down side, the menu hasn't changed much over time and the atmosphere can be a little pretentious. Expect to pay B$175 for two courses before drinks.

Daphne's — *boring menu — expensive.*

Paynes Bay ☎ 432 2731. Daily 12.30–3pm & 6.30–9.30pm. Elegant waterside restaurant turning out delicious Italian–Caribbean fusion food. Try interesting starters like endive, pear, walnut and pecorino salad or smoked marlin carpaccio (B$25–39) and main courses of pork saltimbocca (B$50–60) or several types of pasta, including some interesting vegetarian options such as pumpkin-and-amaretti tortelli (B$39–75).

Fish Pot

Little Good Harbour ☎ 439 2604. Daily 11am–3pm and 6–10pm. Located in a coral stone house with ocean views, *Fish Pot's* menu showcases ambitious and unusual starters such as calamari with pesto-and-crab mousse or fried goujon of alligator for B$26–34, and time-tested main courses of lamb shank, pan-fried barracuda or sauteed shrimp for B$48–70.

Fisherman's Pub

Queen Street, Speightstown ☎ 422 2703. Daily 11am–10pm, live music Wed 6–11pm. A firm area favourite, with a large veranda jutting out over the ocean and the best-value food in town. You can lunch on flying-fish cutters and various types of stew (and sometimes cou-cou) for around B$15–20; dinner is served only on Wednesdays, when B$35 buys you a Bajan feast with accompanying steel pan music and limbo dancing.

La Mer

Port St Charles ☎ 419 2000. Tues–Sat 6.30–9.30pm, Sun noon–2.30pm. Enjoying an appealing location beside a lagoon full of expensive yachts, the food at *La Mer* is simple and well prepared, with main courses like miso-rubbed yellowfin tuna and herb-crusted lamb for B$58–76. The Sunday brunch (B$125) is not to be missed: a magnificent smorgasbord, it includes a carvery and sushi bar.

Lone Star

Mount Standfast ☎ 419 0599. Daily 11.30am–10.30pm. One of the trendiest of the west coast dining spots, drawing a relatively young crowd and lots of expats. The ocean vistas are spectacular and the vibe relaxed, but apart from the caviar, the food is surprisingly downmarket, with shepherd's pie, Indian baltis and tikka masalas, and a three-course Sunday roast all catering to largely British tastes. Main courses B$55–70.

Mango's By the Sea

Speightstown ☎ 422 0704. Daily 6–9.45pm. Classy favourite by the ocean offering friendly service and great local cooking. The extensive menu features starters like an incredible lobster bisque or blackened shrimp for B$19–32, and main courses of fresh fish, ribs and filet mignon for B$49–88. The passion-fruit cheesecake (B$18) is a sensational way to finish.

▼ MANGO'S BY THE SEA

The Mews

2nd Street, Holetown ☎432 1122.
Daily 6.30–11pm. Top-notch food
is served at this Holetown
townhouse – ask for a table on
one of the upstairs terraces. The
seafood dishes are imaginative
and flavoursome – try fresh
dolphin fish poached in
lemongrass, ginger and cilantro,
or shrimp green curry – and the
place is often packed with local
bigwigs. Reckon on B$20–30
for starters, B$50–70 for main
courses. There is also a good
wine list.

Olive's Bar & Bistro

2nd Street, Holetown ☎432 2112.
Daily 6.30–midnight. Popular
Holetown eatery, simple
in design with its wooden
floor and white tablecloths,
but offering a wide choice
of excellent meals. Regular
starters include chicken-
liver parfait or chicken satay
(B$25–30), with main courses
of jerk pork with herb crust
and shrimp curry for around
B$60. The upstairs bar is one
of the best west coast venues
for an early evening drink or a
late-night chill.

Patisserie Bistro Flindt

1st Street, Holetown ☎432 2626.
Mon–Fri 7am–6pm, Sat 7am–2pm,
Sun 7am–noon. Upmarket bakery/
patisserie selling sandwiches,
wraps, salads and pasta (B$22–
34), as well as home-made
breads and mouth-watering
cakes and pastries. The outside
patio next to the main road has
plenty of tables with umbrellas
for shade, but can be noisy.

Ragamuffins

1st Street, Holetown ☎432 1295.
Sun–Fri 6.30–10pm. Colourful,
unpretentious and longstanding
chattel house restaurant serving
reliable Caribbean food. Starters
run B$15–24, while main
courses such as fresh fish, West
Indian curries or jerk-chicken
salad will set you back B$40–55.
There's a drag show on Sunday
evenings that's free if you're
having dinner (reserve a table in
advance) or B$20 if not.

The Tides

Holetown ☎432 8356. Mon–Fri noon–
2.30pm & 6.30–9pm, Sat 6.30–9pm.
One of the west coast's finest
restaurants, best visited in the
evening to take full advantage of

▼ RAGAMUFFINS

the romantic oceanfront tables. Start your meal with dishes like lobster-and-mushroom risotto or foie gras (B$21–50), then move on to shrimp with a spicy banana salsa or scallops with pumpkin-and-pesto risotto (B$60-70). Don't leave without taking a look at the colourful artwork on the walls.

Bars

Coach House

Paynes Bay ☎432 1163. Daily noon–3pm and 6–10.30pm, live music 8pm–2am. This bustling place recreates the traditional English pub, with indoor and outdoor bars. It often has live bands (steel pan every Saturday night), and you can watch English and American sports beamed in by satellite. The food is fine, though nothing to write home about – barbecued chicken, jerk pork, snapper or fresh dolphin for around B$40–50, and curry on Friday nights for B$38.

Crocodile's Den

Paynes Bay ☎432 7625. Daily 5pm–late; karaoke Tues, Thurs & Sun. Funky cocktail bar with pool tables, darts, karaoke and a great late-night atmosphere. This is usually where everyone heads to when the other bars close down for the night.

Mannie's Suga Suga Beach Bar

Mullins Bay ☎419 4511 or 422 3892. Mon–Wed & Fri–Sat 8am–11pm, Thurs & Sun 8am–7pm. One of the busiest bars on the west coast, *Mannie's* also has good, if rather pricey, all-day dining at tables on a wide beachfront veranda. The menu combines Caribbean favourites like pepperpot with

▲ MANNIE'S SUGA SUGA BEACH BAR

sushi, Thai and other Asian-influenced dishes for around B$50.

Marshalls

Holders Hill, opposite the playing field. Daily noon–2pm & 5–9pm. This easy-going local bar serves a wide selection of dishes for around B$15 – try the curried chicken, flying fish or stewed beef, all served with rice and peas, macaroni pie and salad. Though 1.5km inland, *Marshalls* is an essential stop for cricket fans – the owner is cricket-mad, the walls are papered with memorabilia and former players are regular guests.

Surfside Beach Bar

Holetown, behind the police station ☎432 2105. Daily 9am–midnight. A buzzing beach bar that's popular from morning to night, with egg-and-bacon breakfasts (B$13), lunches of sandwiches (B$11–18), pasta or fish and chips (B$23), and dinner options like lasagna, fresh fish or a seafood platter (B$32–39). There's also a daily happy hour (4.30–5.30pm), sports on satellite TV and steel pan music on Sunday evenings.

Central Barbados

The landscape of the quiet central parishes of St George and St Thomas is almost uniformly flat or gently rolling – perfect for the sugar crop that's been under cultivation here for almost four centuries. North of here towards the parish of St Andrew, however, the land rises in a short series of peaks, culminating at the island's highest point, Mount Hillaby. Despite its relatively small area, central Barbados boasts a variety of land-based attractions. Two, Welchman Hall Gully and Turner's Hall Woods, provide a unique glimpse of the island in its primal state; both have been little disturbed since the island was first visited by Europeans. There are negligible facilities here, though, and nowhere to really base yourself, so it's best to visit the middle of the island as a day trip.

St George's Parish Church

The Glebe. Daily 9am–4pm. Free.
Five kilometres or so northeast of Bridgetown, and south of Highway 3, lies St George's Parish Church. Originally built

Getting there and around

Getting to and around the interior of Barbados is straightforward – **buses** from Bridgetown run to the main attractions, though don't count on more than about one departure per hour. The Shorey Village bus from Bridgetown's Princess Alice Bus Station passes many of the sights described in this chapter. However, you'll save a lot of time (and be able to do a lot more exploring) if you rent a car for a day or two – a network of country lanes crisscrosses the island's centre, offering easy access from all coasts (see p.128 for a list of rental agencies).

Signal stations

Gun Hill was one of a chain of six **signal stations** that were quickly constructed on high ground across Barbados after the island's first and only mass slave revolt in 1816 (see p.82). In the era before the telephone, semaphore flags and lanterns were the fastest means of communication over long distances. The stations could rapidly pass signals between the east and west coasts; within minutes of trouble in even the remotest part of the island, the garrison in Bridgetown could be put on alert, or have soldiers marching out to quell any trouble. The stations were also designed to warn of the arrival of enemy ships. However, neither domestic revolt nor enemy invasion ever took place, and the semaphore signals were only ever used to advise of the safe arrival of cargo and passenger ships. With the introduction of the telephone in the late nineteenth century, the stations became unnecessary, and were eventually abandoned in 1887. Today, only two other signal stations still survive in Barbados: the Cotton Tower in St Joseph (see p.119) and Grenade Hall in the north of the island (see p.110).

in the 1630s, this parish church, like all of the island's other old wooden churches, was destroyed in the ferocious hurricane of 1780. The present building dates from 1784, making it the oldest complete church in the country. With its Georgian arched windows and doors, and Gothic buttresses and battlements, the church is a unique architectural hybrid. Inside, the altar painting of the resurrection, *Rise to Power,* by Benjamin West, is one of the best church paintings on the island, while elsewhere are several fine marble commemorative sculptures made in England, including a tablet by Richard Westmacott, sculptor of the statues of Nelson in Trafalgar Square, London and in Bridgetown. The airy chancel is notable for its attractive series of stained-glass windows illustrating biblical scenes. Outside, the extensive cemetery, where old tombs crumble beneath various types of palm, offers a shady stroll and lovely views.

Gun Hill Signal Station

Gun Hill ☏ 429 1358. Mon–Sat 9am–5pm. B$9.20. About a

▲ GUN HILL SIGNAL STATION

kilometre north of St George's Parish Church, Gun Hill Signal Station sits among pretty landscaped gardens. Built in 1818 and impressively restored by the Barbados National Trust in recent years, the watchtower offers fabulous panoramic views across the gently rolling green hills of central Barbados and the ocean beyond Bridgetown. There is a small but immaculate display of military memorabilia, including flags of the various army regiments that were stationed here, maps of the island's many forts – 23 of them had been built as early as 1728 – and the cannons (never fired) that would have alerted the population to enemy invasion. Below the station, and visible from the tower, is a giant white lion – a British military emblem carved from a single block of limestone by soldiers stationed here in 1868.

Orchid World

Highway 3B ☎ 433 0306. Daily 9am–5pm, last entry 4.15pm. B$17.50 or B$25.70 including The Flower Forest.

A kilometre and a half northeast of Gun Hill Signal Station, Orchid World is a stunning collection of around 20,000 of the beautiful flowers displayed among lovely coral rock gardens. Built on an old chicken farm and surrounded by fields of

sugar cane, it's a pretty place – including bougainvillea, ferns, palms and a waterfall – that will take you no more than a comfortable hour to wander around. However, this is one of several botanical attractions on the island, and unless you're an orchid enthusiast, you'll probably find The Flower Forest (see p.106) and Andromeda Botanical Gardens (see p.120) more interesting.

Harrison's Cave

Welchman Hall ☎ 438 6640, ⓦ www .harrisonscave.com. 40min tours daily 9.30am–4pm. B$30. If you follow Highway 2 out of Bridgetown, the first attraction you'll come to is Harrison's Cave (buses stop directly opposite the signposted turn-off for the cave). In this enormous subterranean labyrinth, underground streams and dripping water have carved huge limestone caverns filled with strangely shaped calcite formations. Visitors are taken underground and around the various chambers on an electric tram, which, with the guide's mechanical voice-over, rather spoils the eerie, otherwise soundless atmosphere of the place, though it doesn't detract from the beauty. A twelve-metre waterfall plunges into one of the smaller caves, while a river pours silently through another. Keep an eye out for some of the shapes made by the dripping limestone: the pope, a mother and child, and a flock of vultures.

Welchman Hall Gully

Welchman Hall ☎ 426 2421. Mon–Sat 9am–5pm. B$11.50. On the west side of Highway 2, north from Harrison's Cave, dramatic Welchman Hall Gully is a long, deep corridor of jungle, hemmed in by steep

▲ PALM FRONDS

▲ SUGAR CANE

cliffs and full of local flora and fauna. Though a handful of non-indigenous plants have appeared over the years, today's vegetation is not dissimilar to that which covered the whole island when the British first arrived.

There are two entrances to the gully – one at either end – and buses from Bridgetown stop outside both (the southern entrance is opposite the turn-off for Harrison's Cave; for the northern entrance, continue up Highway 2 and turn left when you reach *Judy's Watering Hole* (rum shop). A marked trail (1km) runs through the gully, past fruit and spice trees dangling with lianas, clove and fig trees, as well as numerous ginger lilies, ferns and palms. Keep an eye out for green monkeys, which are often spotted in the undergrowth during the early morning or late afternoon.

At the time of writing, the future of Welchman Hall Gully was uncertain. Call the Barbados National Trust (☎426 2421) for an update before you set out on a visit.

Springvale Eco-Heritage Museum

Highway 2 ☎438 7011 or 437 9400. Mon–Sat 10am–3.30pm. B$10. A couple of minutes down the hill from *Judy's Watering Hole* brings you to this small folk museum. Besides a collection of locally made furniture, there are traditional Bajan cooking pots and exhibits on the mining of manjak, which is known as "Barbados tar". Browse the extensive library or take a stroll through the pleasant grounds; once part of a sugar plantation, they are now home to a diverting nature trail that leads to an old manjak mine. The museum café serves cakes and soft drinks, including traditional mauby, made from boiling pieces of a bitter tree bark with spices like aniseed and cinnamon.

The Flower Forest

Richmond, signposted just south of Highway 2 ☎ 433 8152. Daily 9am–5pm. B$17.50 or B$25.70 including Orchid World (see p.104).

A little further north from the Springvale Eco-Heritage Museum lies the entrance to the immaculately landscaped Flower Forest. Here you'll find a great variety of indigenous and imported plants and trees, all labelled with both their Latin and English names, as well as country of origin. There are also some fabulous views over the hills of the Scotland District.

The garden, divided into sections with names like "Don's Downhill", "Colin's Corner" and "Mary's Meadow", takes about half an hour to walk through by way of a path that runs around their borders. A seemingly endless list of trees includes breadfruit, coffee, Barbados cherry, avocado and a single African baobab tree, among others, and there is a fine collection of orchids, hibiscus and the "lobster claw" heliconias as well. Another highlight is the Palm Walk, where dozens of different types of palm are scattered around, making for a pleasant, shady place to cool off with a picnic and a good book.

Overall, though, the place feels just a little bit too neat and ordered. If you only have time to visit one of the island's botanical gardens, you're probably better off making for the more rugged Andromeda Botanical Gardens on the east coast (see p.120), though The Flower Forest is certainly worth a look if you're in the area.

Mount Hillaby

At 335m, Mount Hillaby is the highest point in Barbados, and boasts suitably commanding views of the island. To get there, continue north on Highway 2 from The Flower Forest and turn left at the village of Baxters – a sharp uphill beside a faded pink chattel house – and follow the road straight through to the pretty little village of Hillaby. (The road may be covered in markings for **road tennis** – a Bajan invention, formerly known as poor man's tennis and played with paddle bats and a tennis ball to table-tennis rules on a six-metre by three-metre court.) Turn left by the church, past the mini mart, and go another kilometre or so to the end of the road, where you can park. From here, you can look out over the Atlantic-lashed east coast, or take the grassy and sometimes overgrown path on the right that leads to the **summit** and more panoramic views.

Turner's Hall Woods

Near St Simons. Free. This is the only area of Barbados still covered in primary rainforest. As soon as you set foot in the woods, which cover about fifty acres, the humidity makes you aware that you have entered a radically different ecosystem. There's no particular target to make for, but you're free to follow the track (once a proper road) that leads through the centre of the woods. It's a fascinating and verdant place to wander – you'll be surrounded by bird life and ancient vegetation, such as lianas, mahogany trees, jack-in-the-box trees (this is the only place on the island where they grow) and some magnificent silk-cotton trees.

To get to Turner's Hall, take the signposted left off Highway

▲ CHALKY MOUNT POTTERIES

2 to St Simons – about 1.5km north of the Baxters turn-off and soon after you pass Haggatts Government Agriculture Station. Follow the side road through St Simons and right to the end of the track, where you can park a hundred metres from the entrance to the woods.

Chalky Mount Potteries

Chalky Mount. Back on Highway 2 and signposted to the right is Chalky Mount, the highest peak on a range of hills famous for its reddish-brown clay. Potters have operated in the area for generations, and the small village of Chalky Mount – a short hike from the summit – still counts a handful of artisans among its residents. They make and sell sensibly priced mugs, pots and "monkey jugs", traditionally used for keeping drinking water cool. If you can't make it up here, you'll find the same types of pieces at the Pelican Craft Centre in Bridgetown (see p.58) and Earthworks Pottery near Holetown (see p.88).

Belleplaine, Shorey and Cattlewash

Beyond Chalky Mount, Highway 2 continues to the small and wholly untourised town of Belleplaine and the tiny village of Shorey, where the **Conrad Hunte Cricket Club** (named for one of Barbados's greatest cricketers) boasts the island's remotest pitch, with the Atlantic Ocean glistening behind it. If you turn right at Belleplaine, you'll be on the east coast road (officially called the Ermy Bourne Highway), which runs along the eastern edge of the Scotland District through Barclays Park and south to Cattlewash, a tiny village that derives its name from the traditional practice among local farmers of driving their cows down to the sea. If you continue south from here, you'll reach Bathsheba (see p.119).

The north

Although the north of Barbados is the most rugged and least visited part of the island, it nonetheless offers an excellent variety of places to explore. The most popular destination is the Barbados Wildlife Reserve, which is home to hundreds of green monkeys and a host of other animals as well; at nearby Grenade Hall there's an old signal station and a nature trail through the forest. Other specific attractions include a working sugar mill at Morgan Lewis, a superb Jacobean great house, St Nicholas Abbey, and some dramatic cliff-top scenery in the northerly parish of St Lucy. There are no hotels or restaurants along this stretch of coastline; the closest you'll find are over in Speightstown, on the west side of the island.

Barbados Wildlife Reserve

Farley Hill, just north of Highway 2 ☎ 422 8826. Daily 10am–5pm. B$23, including access to Grenade Hall. This wildlife reserve, just off Highway 2 (the Speightstown-to-Bathsheba

▼ BARBADOS WILDLIFE RESERVE

bus stops next to the entrance) was originally established in 1985 for the conservation of **green monkeys** and – more controversially – the possibility of exporting them for medical research. Not long after opening, the idea of turning the reserve into a tourist attraction developed and other creatures were gradually introduced, including brocket deer, which normally hide in the undergrowth, otters, armadillos, mongooses and caiman alligators, as well as caged parrots, macaws and other fabulously coloured tropical birds. Be sure to stop by the information centre, at the northeast corner of the

Getting there and around

Buses run through the northern parishes from both Speightstown and Bridgetown, though, as with services to the central part of the island, there is typically not more than about one departure an hour. The bus that leaves Speightstown for Bathsheba travels along Highway 2, passing directly in front of several of the sights mentioned in this chapter. However, if you're planning to visit more than one of the main attractions – and you could comfortably see all of them in a day – renting a car will make getting around a lot less hassle.

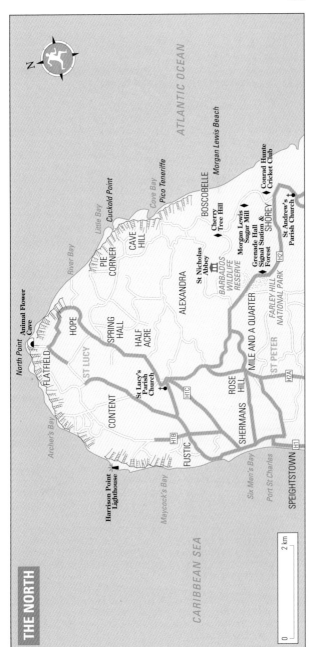

reserve, which has excellent displays on the monkeys and other animals.

Paths meander through the lush mahogany woods; you'll be able to see pretty much everything on offer during a thirty-minute stroll, including the aviary, fishponds, birdcages and plenty of wildlife. The monkeys are definitely the reserve's highlight. They roam about freely, and you can sometimes see them making a break for the outside, leaping from trees over the perimeter fence; apparently, they always return. Don't try to get too close – they can inflict a nasty bite if provoked – and bear in mind that they are not averse to snatching cameras or bags if they are accessible. During the breeding season (Sept–June), the monkeys habitually leave the reserve in the early morning, returning at around 2pm or 3pm. If you plan to visit during these months, try to come in the late afternoon to maximize your chances of seeing them. In the event that you see none, get your ticket stamped and you'll be allowed another free visit at any time within the following two weeks.

Grenade Hall Signal Station and Forest

Farley Hill, next to Barbados Wildlife Reserve ☎ 422 8826. Daily 10am–5pm. B$23, including access to Barbados Wildlife Reserve. The Grenade Hall Signal Station was one of the chain of communication stations (see box, p.103) built in the years immediately after the 1816 slave revolt. The stations, which communicated via semaphore flags and lanterns, were designed to quickly send news of trouble to the garrison in Bridgetown. Grenade Hall is not as attractively located as Gun Hill (see p.103), though the watchtower offers great views of the surrounding countryside, and it's certainly worth a quick tour if you're in the area. Prints of the British military hang downstairs, along with various bits and pieces belonging to signalmen stationed here – medallions, clay pipes, coins and pottery shards – while upstairs some old semaphore signals

Green monkeys

It is thought that **green monkeys** first came to Barbados from West Africa around 1650, as pets of early slave traders. The primates soon established a firm footing in the island's woods and gullies and, though they haven't spread to the surrounding West Indies, they remain prolific in Barbados. They're shy creatures, but you've a good chance of seeing one (or even a troupe) of the estimated five thousand loping across a road as you drive around the interior of the island.

Predictably, to the fury of local farmers, the monkeys have a liking for many of the island's crops; as a result, a bounty has been offered on their heads (or tails) since 1679. Nowadays, the Primate Research Centre at the Barbados Wildlife Reserve offers a substantial reward if they are delivered alive, so you may see monkey traps scattered around – usually nothing more complex than a banana in a cage.

There is plenty of island folklore about the green monkeys, perhaps most endearingly that – like their human cousins – they bury their dead. Modern zoologists scoff at such suggestions but will, if pressed, admit that skeletons are rarely found.

▲ GRENADE HALL SIGNAL STATION

Farley Hill National Park

Farley Hill, entrance opposite Barbados Wildlife Reserve ☎ 422 3555. Daily 7am–6pm. Free (cars B$3.45). This small, pleasant park sits at the top of a three-hundred-metre cliff with commanding views over the Scotland District. It's a good place to retreat with a picnic once you've finished looking around Grenade Hall. The park is the site of what was once a spectacular great house, built for a sugar baron in 1857 and opulently restored in 1956 when it was used as the setting for the movie *Island in the Sun*, starring Harry Belafonte. Hollywood descended in force, adding an immaculate new gallery, staircase and open veranda, painting the trees to get the "right" colour of leaf, and pumping colossal amounts of precious water into the leaky artificial lake. The place went up in flames only a few years later, leaving the old house completely gutted. No attempt was made to repair the damage, and in 1965 the government bought the land and converted it into a park. Today, the charred coral walls of the rather ghostly mansion form the park's centre, and are surrounded by landscaped lawns and masses of fruit trees.

are on display, though most of them post-date the era of slave revolts and relate to shipping movements. There is also an old-fashioned telephone and a small display on the invention that eventually made the signal stations obsolete.

Below Grenade Hall is a large tract of native forest (same hours and ticket as the signal station) where several kilometres of pathways loop through whitewood, dogwood, mahogany and magnificent silk-cotton trees. The shaded, humid forest is a completely different environment than the open countryside seen from Grenade Hall, and the network of paths is complex enough to make it easy to get lost (albeit briefly). Boards put up along the trails list the names and medicinal values of some of the plants and trees and, back at the entrance, there's a detailed description of traditional "bush medicine". The green monkeys from the Barbados Wildlife Reserve spend a good part of the day in the forest, so keep an eye out for them as you walk.

Morgan Lewis Sugar Mill

Morgan Lewis ☎ 426 2421. Mon–Sat 9am–5pm. B$10. Set amid the crumbling ruins of an old sugar factory – a tall chimney pokes defiantly from overgrown grass – Morgan Lewis Sugar Mill is the only windmill in Barbados still in operation. The island once boasted more than five hundred such mills, but mechanization has all but eliminated them from the countryside. The Morgan Lewis Mill, though not an essential stop during your stay in Barbados, provides a unique and instructive insight into this part of the island's history.

Though no longer in commercial use, the mill – first built in the nineteenth century – is still in perfect working order; indeed, the sails, wheelhouse and British-made machinery have been thoroughly restored in recent years. During reaping season (Feb–June), volunteers show how the thick cane stems were pushed through mechanical grinders to extract juice. This demonstration usually takes place on one Sunday per month; for precise dates, call the Barbados National Trust on ☎426 2421. During the rest of the year, there's a small display on the history of the island's mills and a short video showing the Morgan Lewis Mill operating.

▼ CHERRY TREE HILL

Morgan Lewis Beach

The strong undercurrents at this remote spot make swimming here highly dangerous, though the beach itself is a decent place to chill out for an hour or two before you continue touring.

To get here, head uphill from Morgan Lewis Sugar Mill, then turn onto a narrow road for a kilometre to the first houses of Boscobelle. Make a sharp right down a rutted but passable track that eventually leads to the grassy, windblown slopes above Morgan Lewis Beach. There's rarely anyone around and there are no houses in sight.

Cherry Tree Hill

Heading north from Morgan Lewis Sugar Mill, the main road sweeps uphill past sugar-cane fields before reaching a magnificent canopy of mahogany trees at Cherry Tree Hill. It's worth stopping to look behind you across the east coast and out to the Atlantic Ocean for one of the most spectacular views on the island. There is actually no record of cherry trees ever having existed here; local legend has it that they were all chopped down because passers-by kept stealing the fruit, though it sounds a bit unlikely.

St Nicholas Abbey

Cherry Tree Hill ☎422 8725, ⓦwww.stnicholasabbey.com. Daily 10am–3.30pm. B$25. If you continue west from Cherry Tree Hill, after a kilometre or so you'll come to the entrance to St Nicholas Abbey, the oldest house in Barbados and one of only three Jacobean plantation houses left standing in all of the Americas (the others are the privately owned Drax Hall, also in Barbados, and a castle in Virginia, in the

US). Built during the 1650s, the white-painted house with its distinctive ogee gables was originally owned by two of the island's wealthiest sugar-growers. It didn't acquire its present name until the early nineteenth-century, when new owners arrived from St Nicholas Parish in Bristol, England. The origins of its title as an abbey are unknown.

Both the house and grounds, including the small sugar factory next to the house, were recently completely restored. Included in the entrance fee is a guided tour of the ground floor of the house (the upstairs is still used, although there are plans to open some of the rooms), which is crammed with eighteenth-century furniture, Wedgwood porcelain and other traditional accoutrements of the old Barbadian aristocracy. The outbuildings at the back of the house are rather more rustic – the original bathhouse, with its four-seater toilet, remains pretty much intact. A set of old stables have been converted into a rum-bottling house where you can see the spirit being stored and bottled. At the house, you can buy both the rum and molasses from the on-site factory.

Available for viewing is an evocative twenty-minute black-and-white film with some great footage of the boats arriving at Bridgetown harbour and of the pre-war city, with its horse-drawn carts and early cars.

Cove Bay

A couple of kilometres northeast of St Nicholas Abbey lies one of the most beautiful of a series of coves on the island's north coast. Local hustlers may offer to help you find Cove Bay in return for an unspecified tip, but you shouldn't have any trouble finding it on your own: head through Cave Hill to Pie Corner, where a signposted right turn takes you out to the bay.

If you're desperate to swim, you can clamber down to the small, stony beach, but the water is rough and you'll probably want to wait until you're somewhere calmer. The view is the cove's real draw – elegant rows of palm trees stand just above the water's edge, buffeted by the trade winds, and you can see down the entire length of the east coast. To the right, a white cliff rising up to a sharp point 76m above the sea is rather grandly known as Pico Teneriffe.

Little Bay

North of Cove Bay, Little Bay is a rocky, foam-sprayed spot where the surf has carved caves, tunnels and arches into the cliffs. Like the rest of the coast, it's not a great place to swim, but at low tide there are plenty of pools to explore and you can clamber out to look around the caves. Leatherback turtles occasionally crawl onto the beach here to bury their eggs, though your chances of seeing them or their trails are pretty remote.

River Bay

Continuing north, River Bay takes its name from a stream that runs out to the sea through a small, steep-sided valley. It's a popular weekend spot with Bajans, who drive up here for a picnic, and when the water is high it's a pleasant enough place to swim.

Animal Flower Cave

North Point ☎ 439 8797. Daily 9am–4pm. B$10. Right at the barren,

▲ ANIMAL FLOWER CAVE

and filter-feeding tube worms (the "animal flowers") wave their little tentacles about. Early visitors like English clergyman Griffith Hughes collected the "flowers" in the 1740s, taking specimens home to supply mini-museums. Though the numbers of the "flowers" have been heavily depleted since Hughes's day, and do not live up to the advertising hype, the cave remains eerie and slightly surreal.

rocky northern tip of the island, the rather spooky Animal Flower Cave has been a tourist attraction for centuries. Created by the battering of thousands of years of Atlantic waves, the cave is necessarily out of bounds when the sea is rough, and you may want to call ahead if the weather is at all dubious.

A guide takes visitors into the cave, clambering down some stairs and across a slippery floor overhung with stalactites and filled with sinkholes and rockpools, in which a handful of tiny but colourful sea anemones

Archer's Bay

A rocky path west of Animal Flower Cave leads down to a small sandy beach at Archer's Bay – a popular local spot, signposted off the main highway, but often too rough for swimming. Heading south from here, the road leads down to the unremarkable and usually locked St Lucy's Parish Church.

▲ NORTH POINT

The east coast

A handful of small but distinctive places on the surf-lashed and little-touristed east coast offer a change of pace from the built-up south and west of the island. Unless you're really looking to get away from it all, you probably won't want to spend your entire trip here, but it's a great, quiet spot to unwind for a couple of days, walking on the deserted beaches and escaping the crowds. If you don't spend a night or two in the area, try to at least stop for lunch at one of the excellent restaurants around laid-back Bathsheba, or come early in the morning for one of the spectacular east coast sunrises.

Ragged Point

Highway 5 runs east across Barbados from Bridgetown, terminating at the easternmost edge of the island. The main road then veers north (as Highway 4B), passing Ragged Point. Atlantic breakers pound the limestone cliffs here in one of the wildest and most isolated spots on Barbados. On a nearby peninsula stands the disused East Point Lighthouse, one of the main landmarks on this side of the island and a site providing dramatic views up the coast.

Codrington College

Sealy Hall ☎423 1140, ⊛www.codrington.org. College grounds daily 24hr, college buildings Mon–Sat 9am–4pm. Free. Following the main road past Ragged Point, turn right at Blades Hill and continue north to the handsome buildings of Codrington College. The place is named after Christopher Codrington, a wealthy Barbadian landowner and governor of the Leeward Islands from 1698 to 1702. Built in 1743, this was the first degree-level institution established in the English-speaking West Indies; it continues to teach theology to budding Anglican vicars, and is now an affiliate of the University of the West Indies.

▲ RAGGED POINT

Getting there and around

People will often tell you to go to Speightstown to catch a **bus** to Bathsheba. This will be more convenient for those staying on the west coast, but visitors coming from the south coast will find that buses also leave from the Fairchild Street Bus Station in Bridgetown. While getting to Bathsheba is easy, if you want to explore elsewhere in this part of the island it's far more practical to rent a car.

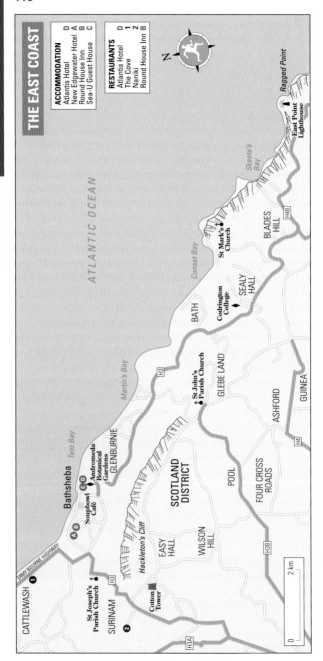

THE EAST COAST

ACCOMMODATION
Atlantis Hotel	D
New Edgewater Hotel	A
Round House Inn	B
Sea-U Guest House	C

RESTAURANTS
Atlantis Hotel	D
The Cove	1
Naniki	2
Round House Inn	B

ATLANTIC OCEAN

Ragged Point
East Point Lighthouse

Skeete's Bay

Conset Bay

St Mark's Church

BLADES HILL

H4B

SEALY HALL

Codrington College

BATH

Martin's Bay

Tent Bay

H3

St John's Parish Church

GLEBE LAND

ASHFORD

GUINEA

H4

Andromeda Botanical Gardens

GLENBURNIE

Bathsheba

Soupbowl Café

Hackleton's Cliff

SCOTLAND DISTRICT

POOL

FOUR CROSS ROADS

H3B

EASY HALL

WILSON HILL

Cotton Tower

SURINAM

H3

St Joseph's Parish Church

CATTLEWASH

ERMY BOURNE HIGHWAY

H3A

0   2 km

▲ CODRINGTON COLLEGE

The approach to the college is dramatic, a long avenue lined on either side with a graceful row of tall cabbage palms and ending beside a large ornamental lake covered in waterlilies. The buildings are arranged around an unfinished quadrangle, with an arched central portico that opens onto large, elegant gardens offering panoramic views over the coast. The modest chapel is on your right as you enter, and the main hall, displaying a bust of Codrington, on your left. The principal's lodge, on the north side of the college, was originally the great house of a sugar plantation; though damaged by fire and hurricane, parts of the seventeenth-century structure remain intact, including the coral stone porch and carved Jacobean balustrades. A stone's throw to the west, a short nature trail has been laid out through the woods – a peaceful place to wander for fifteen minutes or so.

Bath

A little further north from Codrington College, the tall, overgrown chimney of the ruined Bath sugar factory to the right marks the turn-off for this brown-sand beach. It's one of the safest places to swim on the east coast, backed by thick

groves of casuarina trees and protected offshore by a long stretch of coral reef that makes it ideal for snorkelling. There's a children's play area, picnic tables by the water and, on weekends and holidays, a steady stream of Bajans coming to splash around and play beach cricket.

Back on the main road, you'll pass the giant satellite dish that keeps the island in touch with the outside world.

Martin's Bay

Continuing north, the main road meanders along the coastline, past large sugar and banana plantations, en route to the small fishing village of Martin's Bay, nestled on the coast beneath Hackleton's Cliff (see p.118). The village makes a good starting point for a hiking tour of the coast. One appealing

▼ MARTIN'S BAY

walk is between Martin's Bay and Bath; most of it follows a trail along an old railway right-of-way, though at one point you'll have to cut inland around an abandoned rail bridge.

St John's Parish Church

Glebe Land. Daily 9am–5pm. Free. A small road heads directly south from Martin's Bay towards St John's Parish Church. Like many of Barbados's parish churches, St John's – typically English in style with arched doors and windows and a graceful tower – was first built in the mid-seventeenth century but had to be rebuilt following the great hurricane of 1831. The floor of the church is paved with ancient memorial tablets dating back as far as the 1660s and rescued from earlier versions of the building, and a Madonna and child sculpture by Richard Westmacott stands to the left of the main entrance. Most attractive of all is the reddish-brown pulpit, superbly hand-carved from four local woods (mahogany, ebony, manchineel and locust) as well as imported oak and pine. Outside, the expansive graveyard is perched on top of the cliff, looking down over miles of jagged coastline and crammed with moss-covered tombs, family vaults and a wide array of tropical flora.

Hackleton's Cliff and the Scotland District

From St John's Parish Church, follow the road north; after a kilometre or so, a sign diverts you right to Hackleton's Cliff. This steep 300m limestone escarpment marks the edge of the Scotland District to the west and the rugged east coast. At the end of a short track, you can park near the edge of the cliff for fabulous

▼ SCOTLAND DISTRICT

Last of the Byzantines

One of the oldest tombs in the St John's graveyard is that of **Ferdinand Paleologus**, thought to have been the final surviving descendant of the brother of Constantine XI – the last emperor of the Byzantine Greeks – who was killed in battle when present-day Istanbul was captured by the Turks in 1453. Ferdinand's family moved to England, where he grew up, and he fought for King Charles I during the English Civil War. Like many defeated Royalists, he fled to Barbados in 1646, where he became a churchwarden of St John's and, later, a lieutenant in the militia.

Ferdinand's coffin was originally placed in a vault under the choir, facing the opposite direction to the other coffins (with the head pointing west) and with the large skeleton embedded in quicklime, both customs of the Greek Orthodox Church. After the 1831 hurricane it was moved to the churchyard where it remains today. During the Greek War of Independence in the 1820s, the provisional Greek government made enquiries in Barbados to see if there was any surviving male descendant of Ferdinand who might return as a figurehead for their new battle with the Turks. None was found.

▲ COTTON TOWER

views across the craggy hills of the Scotland District, nostalgically labelled by early settlers for its supposed resemblance to the country of the same name, and up the sandy northeast coastline. It's a peaceful spot, where the only sound is often the calling of the swifts as they wheel away on the warm currents of air rising from the ground hundreds of metres below.

The Cotton Tower

Bowling Alley Hill. If you follow the road that runs northwest parallel to Hackleton's Cliff, you'll pass through the tiny village of Easy Hall and past the derelict remains of Buckden

▼ WEATHER-BEATEN HOUSE, BATHSHEBA

Great House – which is overgrown and rather eerie with plants pushing up through the floorboards and green monkeys scampering around on the dilapidated roof – and eventually see the pink Cotton Tower on the left. Built in 1819 and named for Lady Caroline Cotton, daughter of the island's governor, this is one of the six signal stations built in the early nineteenth century to warn of slave uprisings or the arrival of enemy boats (see box, p.103). The Cotton Tower has been earmarked for renovation but is presently closed to visitors and rather run-down. Contact the Barbados National Trust at ☎426 2421 for the latest news.

Bathsheba

The road joins Highway 3 just beyond the Cotton Tower. Turn right and go down the hill (the gradient is very steep towards the end) to Bathsheba. Picturesque, laid–back and caressed by Atlantic breezes, this has long been a favoured resort for Bajans, though surprisingly few tourists make it up here. Small holiday homes and the odd rum shop line the road as it runs beside the sea, but otherwise there is not much else to Bathsheba.

If the bay, dotted with large rocks, looks familiar, it's because this is one of the most painted landscapes in Barbados. Also known as the "**soup bowl**", because of the surf that crashes in here pretty much all year round, the area is a popular surfing spot and the site of several annual tournaments. Surfboards can be rented from a shack in the village called *Soupbowl Café* for B$40 per hour (though it keeps rather irregular hours). Unfortunately, the currents also mean that it's not a good place to swim, but the wide brown beach is attractive and there's an old pathway if you fancy a walk.

For a pleasant hour-long hike, wander between Bathsheba and Cattlewash, slightly to the north (see p.107), along either the beach or the old railway track that passes in front of the *Round House Inn* and *New Edgewater Hotel*; en route, you'll cross Joe's River – one of just two permanently flowing rivers in Barbados – and can cut inland to look at the dense woods bordering it. On returning to Bathsheba, stop for a bite to eat at one of the town's good restaurants.

Andromeda Botanical Gardens

Bathsheba ☏ 433 9384. Daily 9am–5pm, last entry 4.30pm. B$17.50. At the eastern end of Bathsheba, the road gradually veers away from the coast and climbs a steep hill, passing a signposted left turn-off for the *Atlantis Hotel* (see p.121), before arriving at Andromeda Botanical Gardens. These colourful, sprawling gardens are the most attractive on the island, spreading over a hillside strewn with coral boulders and offering fabulous vistas of the coastline. Created by local botanist Iris Bannochie in 1954, the gardens feature masses of native and imported shrubs and plants landscaped around a trail that incorporates several ponds and a giant, ancient bearded fig tree.

The hibiscus garden, on your left as you enter, showcases

▼ SHAVING BRUSH TREE

▲ ATLANTIS HOTEL

every shade of the flower (even a grey hybrid), and is the best place to see the tiny hummingbirds that frequent the botanical gardens. Note that the hibiscus doesn't bloom just after having been cut, so call ahead if the hibiscus garden is the main reason for your visit. Otherwise, trails take you around the gardens and past some old traveller's trees and a small clump of papyrus before turning uphill past a series of brilliant heliconia – including the bizarrely shaped "beefsteak" – and a panama hat tree. The beautiful bearded fig tree, which appears on the national coat of arms and from which the name "Barbados" is derived, is the star attraction, but there are plenty of other highlights, including a bank of frangipani, rose of sharon trees, superb cycads and a *Bombax ellipticum*, also known as the shaving brush tree for its large pink-bristled flowers. At the lower end of the trail, the Queen Ingrid Palm Garden features dozens of types of palm, including the massive tailpot, largest of the fan palms and often used abroad for thatched roofing.

Local botanists offer an entertaining, free guided tour of the gardens each Wednesday at 10.30am. The *Hibiscus Café*, inside the garden, serves light meals as well as delicious Barbadian cherry juice, and there's a small gift shop selling prints, T-shirts, books and bottles of rum.

Accommodation

Atlantis Hotel

Tent Bay ☎433 9445, ⓦwww .atlantisbarbados.com. Built in the 1880s, this was one of the first hotels to be put up outside Bridgetown. Overlooking picturesque Tent Bay, it's a welcoming place whose great food brings people from all around the island. The eight modest rooms all come with bathrooms, but no TV or telephone; ask for one with a balcony. Rooms from US$110/70 in winter/summer.

New Edgewater Hotel

Bathsheba, at the western end ☎433 9900, ⓕ433 9902, ⓦwww .newedgewater.com. A recent change in ownership and large-scale renovations have made the rooms more comfortable, though most still have disappointing views given the hotel's location high above Bathsheba Bay. Rooms 221 (the Honeymoon Suite) and 218 are more expensive, but they are the only ones with balconies overlooking the sea. There's also a pool and a decent restaurant. Rooms from US$121/84 in winter/summer.

Round House Inn

Bathsheba ☎ 433 9678, ⊛ www .roundhousebarbados.com. The owners of this excellent restaurant (see p.123) rent out four clean but basic en-suite rooms upstairs (from US$100/85 in winter/summer), all with access to a communal roof terrace with limited sea views. Satisfactory, but you can find better value for your money at Bathsheba's other hotels.

Sea-U Guest House

Bathsheba ☎ 433 9450, ⊛ www .seaubarbados.com. Pleasant, friendly little German-managed guesthouse next to the *Atlantis Hotel*, surrounded by an acre of tropical garden. The rooms (without TV and telephone) are cosy, the atmosphere relaxed

and the views from the large, hammock-strewn veranda excellent. Probably the best accommodation option on the east coast. Rooms from US$110/74 in winter/summer.

Restaurants

Atlantis Hotel

Bathsheba ☎ 433 9445. Daily 8am–8pm. Faded old hotel with loads of character and great home cooking. The vast Sunday buffet (B$50), featuring traditional Bajan food, is staggeringly good, while the good value weekday prix-fixe menu (B$35) includes a hearty soup, spicy lamb or flying fish and a tasty dessert. The large number of locals present is as good a recommendation as you'll get.

The Cove

Bathsheba ☎ 433 9495. Wed, Thurs, Sat & Sun noon–3pm. Popular with Bajans and well worth

▲ ROUND HOUSE INN

stopping at if you're passing through. The friendly folk at *The Cove* offer tasty lunches that change daily but might include coconut chicken curry or fresh fish, as well as a range of soups and sandwiches. Starters cost B$12–28, main courses B$32–48. Reservations are required for Sunday's Caribbean buffet (B$65) and are recommended on other days if you want a table overlooking the sea.

Naniki

Surinam, signposted west of Highway 3 ☎ 433 1300. Tues–Sun 12.30–3pm. Consider having lunch at this well regarded Caribbean restaurant serving starters such as bol jol, saltfish and crab salad (B$9–33) and mains dishes that could include anything from pepperpot and flying fish to stewed lambie (conch) or,

for vegetarians, stewed soya chunks with root vegetables (B$29–44).

Round House Inn

Bathsheba ☎ 433 9678. Mon–Sat 8am–10pm, Sun 8am–5pm. Enjoy top-quality cooking and a casual, family atmosphere at this excellent restaurant overlooking beautiful Bathsheba Bay. The lunch and dinner menus are similar – with main dishes like blackened catch of the day, shrimp and dolphin (B$48–52) – but it's the original starters such as breadfruit soup and baked rum-nut brie (B$10–26) that really catch the eye. Pretty much the only place for regular live music in the area: there's jazz (Wed), reggae (Sat) and a guitarist (Sun) during winter; just the guitarist during summer.

Essentials

Arrival

All **flights** to Barbados arrive at **Grantley Adams International Airport**, which is located on the south coast about eight miles east of Bridgetown, and is within easy striking distance of all the main south coast resorts. **Buses** run between the airport and Bridgetown roughly every half-hour (B$1.50), stopping at or near most of the south coast resorts en route. Services to the resorts on the west coast are less frequent; look for buses going direct to Speightstown to avoid having to change buses (and terminals)

in Bridgetown. **Taxis** from the airport to Crane Bay cost about B$25, to the resorts on the south coast B$30, to the hotels around Holetown on the west coast B$50 and around Speightstown B$60. For those interested in private transportation, there are numerous **car** rental outlets at the airport.

The occasional **cruise ship** arrives at the Deep Water Harbour just north of Bridgetown; taxis are always available here to ferry passengers around the island.

Information

The **Barbados Tourism Authority** office on Harbour Road in Bridgetown, immediately west of the Pelican Craft Centre (Mon–Fri 8.15am–4.30pm; ☎427 2623, ℉ 426 4080, ⓦ www.barbados .org), can provide visitors with plenty of information on the country, including brochures on the main tourist attractions and a map. They also operate a desk in the baggage claim area at the airport.

While the maps in this book should get you anywhere you want to go, three free maps of Barbados – *Barbados Holiday Map*, *Barbados in a Nutshell* and *Ins & Outs of Barbados* – are available at many hotels, restaurants and other tourist facilities, and are perfectly adequate for most exploring.

Barbados has no detailed listings magazine for music, theatre or cinema, though the free fortnightly magazine *Friends* – available from the tourist office and some hotels – carries local community and tourist news, as well as a listing of what's going on at the island's bars and clubs. The free advertisement-driven publications *Barbados in a Nutshell*, *Ins & Outs of Barbados* and *Barbados Holiday Guide* feature descriptions of tourist attractions and restaurants, but no listings. The Barbados Tourism Authority website carries information on upcoming island events; you can also check the daily papers (see p.142) and local radio stations (see p.143).

Documents and regulations

To enter Barbados, all visitors must have a **passport** valid for at least six months after the date of departure. Citizens of Britain, Ireland, the US, Canada, Australia and New Zealand can enter Barbados without a visa and stay for up to three months, although your passport will be stamped initially for a thirty-day period. On arrival, you'll be asked to present a return ticket or proof of onward travel, and you may also be asked to show that you have sufficient funds to cover your visit. Once in Barbados, to extend the length of your stay, contact the Immigration office in Bridgetown (☎426 9912).

Island transport and tours

Inexpensive, speedy buses and minibuses run around the island's coasts and into almost every nook and cranny of the interior. An even better, though more expensive, way to see Barbados is to rent a car for a couple of days and cruise around at your own pace. If you just want to make the odd excursion or short trip, it can work out cheaper to take a taxi or even to go on a guided tour.

By bus

Blue government **buses** and smaller, privately owned yellow **minibuses** run all over the island. They offer particularly good service along the west coast, between Bridgetown and Speightstown, and along the south coast, between Bridgetown and Silver Sands. The fare is a flat rate of B$1.50; minibuses will give you change, but you'll need the exact money on government buses. Posted with red-and-white signs, bus stops are never far apart, and are marked "To City" and "Out of City", depending on whether the bus is going to or from Bridgetown. A bus's specific destination is written on a board on its front; if it's not clear where you're headed, other passengers will usually be able to help you out.

Privately owned white minivans known as **route taxis** or ZRs (because of the "ZR" on their numberplates) operate like minibuses, packing in passengers and stopping anywhere they see potential riders. Also, like the buses, they're particularly numerous on the south coast, and the fare is B$1.50. Many Bajans don't use route taxis because they consider the drivers to be reckless and totally uninterested in passenger comfort.

By car

Driving in Barbados is fairly easy, and the best option for anyone wanting to do some off-the-beaten-track exploring. The roads are mostly good, and distances between points of interest short, although poor lighting and relatively heavy traffic can make driving at night a bit daunting. Driving is on the left. Rental prices, however, can be high, starting at around B$160 per day or B$550 per week for regular **cars**. Mini **mokes** (the open-sided buggies that you'll see all over the island) cost roughly the same as regular cars, but, unless you really enjoy driving with the wind in your hair, are less comfortable. Third-party **insurance** (protecting against claims by third parties) and collision damage insurance (protecting against damage to the rental car) are normally included in the price, although always check beforehand.

You'll need a local **licence** (issued by the car rental agency for a B$10 fee) to drive in Barbados, in addition to a current licence from your home country or an international driver's licence and, normally, a **credit card** to make a security deposit. Check the car fully to ensure that every dent, scratch or missing part is inventoried before you set off. When returning the car, don't forget to collect any credit card deposit slips.

The large international rental agencies do not operate out of Barbados and, since car rental companies on the island are all local, it can be easier to organize things once you've arrived. Reliable firms include Coconut (☎ 437 0297), Jones (☎ 426 5030), Mangera (☎ 436 0562) and National (☎ 422 0603), or if you want a mini moke, Stoutes (☎ 416 4456). Each of these should deliver the car to your hotel.

Trips to other islands

LIAT (☎434 5428, ⓦwww.liatairline.com) runs **flights** to all the nearby islands as well as into Guyana in South America. Fares start at around B$290 for round-trip flights to St Lucia, B$425 to St Vincent and B$175 to Grenada; most fares include one or more free stopovers en route. Tickets are sold at a multitude of travel agents island-wide.

If you really want to splash out, consider an organized **day trip** to the beautiful Grenadine Islands: you take an early morning flight to Union Island and then a catamaran trip through several of the cays that includes plenty of opportunities for snorkelling and a buffet lunch. Prices start at B$825 per person, rising to B$1250 if you want to stop off at Mustique for breakfast and a tour of the houses of the rich and famous. Contact tour operator Chantours (☎432 5591) for more information.

Although you can occasionally find a company willing to rent **scooters** (but seldom motorcycles), the island's narrow roads make this a risky option and one not really recommended at all.

By taxi

Finding a **taxi** in Barbados – identified by the Z on their numberplates – is rarely a problem. They are particularly recommended if you're travelling around at night, when bus service is minimal and driving is made less desirable by poor lighting and somewhat heavy traffic. The best option is to ask your hotel or guesthouse to recommend a local company; if they can't help, try one of the following. Bridgetown: Independence ☎426 0090; Rockley: Rockley Taxi ☎435 8211; St Lawrence Gap: Chattel House Village Taxi ☎428 1877; Holetown: Sunset Crest ☎432 0367. When calling to order a taxi, avoid a potentially long wait by using a company based close by; numbers are listed in the phone book.

Fares are regulated but there are no meters, so agree on a fee before you get in the car. Most taxi drivers are scrupulously honest, but you might want to check on the appropriate fare to your destination at your hotel before you go.

By bike

Barbados would seem like ideal cycling territory because it is so small, and there are few steep inclines, but this mode of transport has never really caught on. The heat is obviously a factor, as are the often very narrow roads; exercise extreme caution when cycling around the island. **Bike** rental options are limited, although you can normally get a bike from Dread or Dead in Hastings (☎228 4785) for B$40 per day or B$150 per week.

Tours

For those who don't fancy driving themselves, there are various local companies that offer island-wide sightseeing **tours**, either as part of a set itinerary or customized to your interests. Your hotel may also organize tours. Remember to check whether the price you are quoted includes entrance fees to the various attractions. If you can't get a good price from any of the companies below, you could check with some of the taxi operators (see above) or consider taking one of the Sunday Scenic Tours operated by the government-run bus company (see box, p.130).

Tour companies

Bajan Helicopters ☎431 0069, ⓦwww .bajanhelicopters.com. Short but spectacular helicopter tours of the island from the heliport in Bridgetown. A twenty-minute

Sunday Scenic Tours

An excellent and inexpensive way to see some of the lesser-explored parts of the island is on a tour organized by the government-run bus company. Every Sunday a **special bus** operates a route that passes several of the island's main sights, stopping at each one to allow passengers to visit them (entry fees are not included); the route is different each outing. Past destinations have included Foul Bay (see p.80), Bath (see p.117), Cherry Tree Hill (see p.112), Little Bay (see p.113), River Bay (see p.113), Animal Flower Cave (see p.113) and other places that are time consuming to get to without your own transport. Most passengers are Bajan, so the tours can be a great way to meet locals, and the atmosphere is much more low-key than the tours operated mainly for foreign tourists. Buses leave from Independence Square in Bridgetown every Sunday at 2pm and tickets (B$15) can be bought at either the Fairchild Street or Princess Alice bus stations. For more information, call ☎426 8249 and ask for the Marketing & Corporate Communications Department.

ride across the island costs B$280, thirty minutes around the coastline B$360.
Boyce's Tours ☎425 5366, ⊛www .boycestours.com. Offers full- and half-day tours covering all of the island's main sights There's a four-person minimum for each tour. B$20 to B$58, excluding entry fees.
Island Safari ☎429 5337, ⊛www .islandsafari.bb. One of the more organized tour groups, and, with advertisements everywhere, probably the most publicized.

They offer excellent, informative Land Rover cruises of the island – especially the wilder places away from the established "sights" – costing from B$139 to B$325 (including lunch). Prices depend on how much exploring they're doing on a particular day.
Johnson's Tours ☎426 5181, ⊛www .johnsonstours.com. Can provide a car and driver to take you around for B$60 per hour (entry fees extra). There's a maximum of four people per car; larger groups will have to get a minivan, which is twice the price.

Money

Barbados is one of the more expensive countries in the Caribbean, with prices for many items comparable to what you'd pay at home. Negotiation on prices is generally frowned on – taxi fares, for example, are normally fixed – but, particularly during the off-season (May–Nov), it can be worth enquiring about reduced rates for items like accommodation or car rental.

Currency

The island's unit of currency is the **Barbados dollar** (B$), which comes in bills of 2, 5, 10, 20, 50 and 100 dollars, and coins of 1, 5, 10 and 25 cents,

and $1. The rate of exchange is fixed at B$2 to US$1 – though you'll get a fraction less when you exchange money – and the US dollar is usually accepted in payment for goods and services.

In Barbados, prices are normally quoted in B$, with the exception of accommodation, which is almost universally quoted in US$. We have followed this practice in the Guide.

Costs

Apart from your flight, accommodation is likely to be the major expense of your trip. The least expensive double rooms – usually in the guesthouses on the south coast – start at around US$25 (£13/B$50), though most of the cheaper hotels cost around US$100–120 (£54–65/B$200–240) in winter and US$70–80 (£38–43/B$140–160) in summer. Expect to pay US$200 and up (£108/B$400) in winter and over US$100 (£54/B$200) in summer for something more salubrious, and on the west coast. The most luxurious places in that area, meanwhile, often cost in excess of US$600 (£323/B$1200) in winter and US$250 (£135/B$500) in summer.

Rooms apart, if you travel around on public transport, buy your food from supermarkets and eat at the cheaper restaurants, you can just about survive on a daily budget of around US$30 (£16/B$60) per day. Upgrade to one decent meal out, the occasional museum or plantation-house visit and a bit of evening entertainment, and you can expect to spend a more realistic US$50–60 (£27–32/B$100–120); after that, the sky's the limit.

Traveller's cheques, credit cards and ATMs

Easily the safest method of carrying money abroad is in the form of **traveller's cheques**. While sterling and other currencies are accepted in the island's banks, US dollar traveller's cheques are the most convenient ones to have. They are available for a small commission from most banks, and from branches of American Express and Thomas Cook; make sure you keep the purchase agreement and a record of cheque serial numbers safe and separate from the cheques themselves. Once in Barbados, they can be cashed at banks (you'll need your passport or other photo ID to validate them) for a small charge.

Major **credit cards** – American Express, Mastercard, Visa – are widely accepted on the island, though many smaller hotels and restaurants will not take them. You can also use the cards to get cash advances at most banks, though you'll pay both commission to the bank and hefty interest to your credit card company.

Many banks, including Royal Bank of Canada, have **ATMs** that accept all major cards. It's better to use a **debit card** than a credit card for ATM withdrawals, since in the latter's case such withdrawals are treated as cash advances and, therefore also incur high interest charges. However, you will still pay a commission on the money you draw from the machine; the size of the commission varies, depending upon the bank.

Banks and exchange

Banking hours are generally Monday through Thursday 8am to 3pm and Friday 8am to 5pm. Many hotels will also exchange money, though if you're changing anything other than US dollars the rate is usually a bit worse than at a bank.

There is a bureau de change in the baggage claim area at the **airport**, and you'll find a branch of the Barbados National Bank (open to coincide with flight arrivals) and two ATM machines in the departures hall.

Emergency cash

If you run out of money, you can arrange a telegraphic transfer to most of the banks in Barbados from your home bank account or that of a friend or family member. Bear in mind that such a transfer will incur hefty commissions at both ends, so treat this very much as a last resort.

Accommodation

There is no shortage of places to stay in Barbados. Accommodation options run the gamut from some of the world's best hotels to simple and inexpensive guesthouses. You'll find most of the pricier choices along the **west coast**, traditionally the swankier side of the island; many of them are concentrated around lovely Paynes Bay or on either side of Holetown, though they thin out considerably as you continue north towards Speightstown. On the **south coast**, the beaches are just as good (if not better), and accommodation is much more reasonably priced. Good-value options are plentiful, particularly around Worthing and St Lawrence Gap, as well as the windsurfing centres of Maxwell and Silver Sands. There is very little accommodation elsewhere on the island. A handful of small, mostly long-established hotels still do a light trade in Bathsheba on the wild **east coast**, but there is as yet nowhere to stay in the centre or north of the island. There are also no youth hostels on the island and camping is banned.

All-inclusives

Barbados, like many other Caribbean countries, is full of "all-inclusive" hotels. The simple concept behind these places is that you pay a single price that covers your room, all meals and, normally, all drinks and water sports, thus allowing you to "leave your wallet at home".

If you are thinking of booking an all-inclusive, focus on what you specifically want out of it. *Almond Beach* and *Turtle Beach*, for example, have several restaurants and bars, so you don't have to face the same menu every night; smaller places like *Escape* offer less variety, but a bit more space on the beach. Know, too, that the allure of drinking seven types of "free" cocktail in a night or stuffing your face at the "free" buffet can fade quickly; if you want to get out and sample Barbados's myriad great restaurants and bars – and to interact with Bajans – you're better off steering clear of all-inclusives.

Private homes, apartments and villas

A number of families offer bed and breakfast in their homes; the Barbados Tourism Authority (see p.127) can normally provide lists. Rates generally start around US$20 per person. If you're interested in renting a private apartment or villa, Altman Real Estate (℡ 432 0840, Ⓦ www.aaaltman.com) and Ronald Stoute & Sons (℡ 423 6800,

---

Accommodation prices

Since nearly every hotel has a significant difference between its winter, or high, season (mid-Dec to mid-April) rates and its prices in summer (May–Nov), we have given both categories in the Guide, with the winter price first. The rates quoted are for the cheapest double room before tax; for all-inclusive hotels we have stated whether the price is for one or two people. Bear in mind that over the Christmas and New Year period (mid-Dec to early Jan) prices can rise dramatically. At many hotels, if you book for a week or more with a foreign tour operator as part of a package, prices will normally be much lower.

Note that virtually all of the hotels will add a seven percent government tax (VAT) to your bill, while many others will levy a ten percent service charge on top of the VAT. Check whether or not these are included in the price you are quoted when you make your reservation.

ⓦ www.ronstoute.com) have details of properties available; check also ⓦ www.barbadosvillavacations.com. Prices vary greatly depending on amenities, size and location, but reckon on starting prices of around US$150/110 per night for a one-bedroom villa in winter/ summer or US$250/185 per night in winter/summer for a two-bedroom villa. You can, of course, pay in the thousands of dollars per night for sumptuous properties complete with swimming pools, magnificent views and a lot of privacy.

Communications

Calling within Barbados is simple – many hotels provide a **telephone** in each room and local calls are usually free (though check before you place any calls). You'll also see Bartel phone booths all over the island; these can be used for both local and international calls. Most of the booths take phonecards only – these are available at hotels, post offices and some shops and supermarkets. Local calls made from public phones cost 25 cents for five minutes. For finding numbers, hotel rooms and phone booths often have a directory; failing that, call directory assistance on ☎411. To make a **collect call**, dial ☎0 for the overseas operator, who will then connect you.

Mail

Barbados's **postal service** is extremely efficient. The General Post Office in Bridgetown (Mon–Fri 7.30am–5pm) has *poste restante* facilities for receiving mail. There are branch offices across the island in the larger towns and villages, as well as at the airport (Mon–Fri 8am–3.15pm); you can also buy stamps and send mail at many of the hotels. Postal rates are reasonable: letters and postcards sent by air mail to the UK are B$1.75; to the US and Canada, B$1.40.

Email

Many hotels will let you use their computers for free or for a nominal charge if you want to check **email** or surf the Internet. These days, several hotels also have WiFi coverage, so you can get online with your own laptop computer. Alternatively, there are a fair number of Internet cafés dotted around the island: in St Lawrence Gap, *Bean & Bagel* (see p.76) offers Internet access for B$7 for fifteen minutes; in Holetown, Global Business Centre (a stall in the West Coast Mall) charges B$2.50 for five minutes; and in Bridgetown, the General Post Office charges B$3 for fifteen minutes.

Dialling codes

To call Barbados from abroad
Dial your international access code (see below) + 246 + seven digit number
UK ☎001
USA ☎011
Canada ☎011
Australia ☎0011
New Zealand ☎00

To call abroad from Barbados
Dial the country code (see below) + number (omitting the initial zero if there is one)
UK ☎011 44
USA ☎1
Canada ☎1
Australia ☎011 61
New Zealand ☎011 64

Food and drink

As you'd expect, fresh **seafood** is the island's speciality: snapper, tuna, barracuda, dolphin fish (also called mahi mahi or dorado to distinguish it from the mammal), shrimp and lobster are all easy to find. Most popular of all, though, is **flying fish** – virtually a Bajan national emblem. The name is a bit deceptive – the fish don't really fly. Accelerating up to 65kph, they shoot out of the water and, extending their lateral fins like wings, can glide through the air for up to thirty metres.

You'll find traditional Bajan fare on many menus. The national dish is **cou-cou** (a cornmeal and okra pudding) and saltfish, and you'll occasionally encounter the fabulous **pudding and souse** – steamed sweet potato served with cuts of pork pickled in onion, lime and hot peppers. **Cohobblopot** (more widely known as **pepperpot**) is a spicy meat-and-okra stew. Dishes from the wider Caribbean, such as the fiery Jamaican-style jerk pork or chicken, are also popular.

Vegetarians will have to work a bit to avoid meat or fish. Despite the fantastic selection of vegetables available on the island, including the starchy **breadfruit** (best roasted) and the squash-like **christophene**, restaurants often don't have even a single vegetarian option. Though the ubiquitous **peas and rice** (rice cooked with a variety of peas or beans) may sound acceptable to vegetarians, watch out – a piece of salt pork is usually chucked into the pot for added flavour.

Cutters (bread rolls with a meat or cheese filling) and coconut bread are available as snacks in many bars and rum shops, and more substantial **rotis** (flat, unleavened bread wrapped around a filling of curried meat or vegetables) are also served widely. Less frequently seen outside a Bajan home, but worth keeping an eye open for, are **conkies**, made from pumpkin, sweet potato, cornmeal and coconut, all mixed together and steamed in banana leaves.

Finally, don't miss out on the superb local **fruits**, from mangos and paw paws to the more exotic sapodillas and sweet-sops.

Drink

Rum (see box, p.66) is the liquor of choice in Barbados. Hundreds of tiny rum bars, or "shops", dot the island; they are an integral part of Bajan social life, and are great places to stop off for a drink and a chat.

The local **beer** is Banks, a light golden lager made from a blend of barley and hops, by far the most popular brew island-wide. **Wine** is catching on, but remains an expensive option when compared with rum and beer – you'll occasionally find Californian whites and reds at reasonable prices, however. In terms of **bars**, on the west coast you'll find fewer places that cater specifically for drinkers, but all-inclusives apart, most hotels and restaurants will welcome you for a drink even if you're not staying or eating there. St Lawrence Gap and, to a lesser extent, Holetown are particularly good for bar-hopping.

The complete range of soft drinks is available everywhere, as is bottled water, though the tap water in Barbados is among the purest anywhere in the world and perfectly safe to drink.

Festivals, events and public holidays

The main festival in Barbados is the summertime Crop Over (see p.136), which reaches its climax on Kadooment Day when the festival monarchs are crowned. There are plenty of other events to distract you from the beach as well, for which the Barbados Tourism Authority (see p.127) has full details. Alternatively, call the appropriate number or check the websites listed below.

Festival and event calendar

January
Barbados Jazz Festival ☎ 429 2084, ⓦ www.barbadosjazzfestival.com. A prestigious line-up of international jazz musicians and singers perform concerts at indoor and outdoor locations for a week in the middle of the month.

February
Holetown Festival ⓦ www.holetown festivalbarbados.com. Commemorating the first settlement of Barbados at Hole-town in February 1627, the week-long festival showcases local arts and crafts as well as Barbadian culture and history. Events typically include fashion shows,

street parades, concerts and sporting matches.
Carib Beer Cup ☎ 436 1397. The cricketing nations of the Caribbean play in this round-robin competition held from November to February. Barbados is traditionally the most successful team, boasting a total of nineteen victories.

March
Holders Season ☎ 432 6385, ⓦ www .holders.net. From mid-March to early April this festival takes over a refined old plantation house. The focus is on classical music and opera, but the programme often includes music from other genres, theatre and even comedy shows. For more information, see p.88.
Oistins Fish Festival ☎ 427 2623. This annual festival celebrates the town of Oistins' fishing tradition with boat races and fish-boning tournaments.
Test cricket ☎ 436 1397. See p.141.

May
Gospelfest ☎ 426 5128, ⓦ www .barbadosgospelfest.com. This lively festival reflects the important role that gospel music plays in the spiritual lives of many Barbadians. Bringing together some of the top gospel singers and bands from North America, the Caribbean and Barbados, the festival also includes reggae, calypso, jazz and soul.

Public holidays

New Year's Day	Jan 1
Errol Barrow Day	Jan 21
Good Friday	Fri before Easter Sun
Easter Monday	day after Easter Sun
National Heroes Day	April 28
Labour Day	May 1
Whit Monday	eighth Mon after Easter
Emancipation Day	Aug 1
Kadooment Day	first Mon in Aug
United Nations Day	first Mon in Oct
Independence Day	Nov 30
Christmas Day	Dec 25
Boxing Day	Dec 26

July–August

Crop Over Festival ☎ 424 0909,
ⓦ cropover.ncf.bb. Held every summer,
Crop Over celebrates the completion of the
sugar harvest. Alongside the flags, dancing and rum-drinking, the symbol of the
festival is "Mr Harding" – a scarecrow-like
figure stuffed with the dried leaves of the
sugar cane – who is paraded around and
introduced to the managers of the sugar
plantations. Though Crop Over has lost
some of its significance since the 1960s,
with tourism replacing sugar as the country's main industry, it's still the island's best
festival and an excuse for an extended
party. Things really get going in late July
and early August, with street parades and
concerts.

November

**Independence Pro Classic Surfing
Championships** ☎ 228 5117. Held in
Bathsheba's "soup bowl", this is one of
the best regarded surfing competitions
in the Caribbean, attracting professional
surfers from other islands as well as
the US.

**National Independence Festival of
Creative Arts** ☎ 424 0909, ⓦ nifca.ncf
.bb. To celebrate the country's independence, the best singers, dancers, writers
and even chefs in each parish take part
in national competitions. There is no age
limit for contestants, and although the
home-grown talent is at times only average, it's all taken seriously but there is a
fun atmosphere.

December

Run Barbados Road Race Series
☎ 427 2623, ⓦ www.runbarbados.org.
Five separate races take place on the
first Sunday in December: a marathon,
half-marathon, 10km run, 5km walk and
toddlers' walk.

Shopping

If you want to take home something
authentically Bajan, check out the
craft shops at **Pelican Craft Centre**
(see p.58) in Bridgetown. Alternatively,
wait for the vendors to find you – they
hang out on the most popular beaches,
particularly Accra Beach on the south
coast, and regularly set up stands selling
clothing, carved wooden figurines and
Haitian-style paintings of markets and
other traditional scenes. The **Best of
Barbados** gift shops (see p.95) dotted
around the island also sell decent-
quality souvenirs, from books and prints
to T-shirts and rum cake. The most
authentically Bajan souvenir of all is
rum (see p.66), which is available at the
souvenir shops, but cheaper if bought at
the supermarkets.

The vast array of **duty-free shops** lining Broad Street in Bridgetown (mostly
open Mon–Fri 9am–5pm, Sat 9am–1pm)
are always popular. For the widest selection of cigarettes, alcohol, perfume and
the like at the best prices, go to Cave
Shepherd (see p.59). You can buy items
at duty-free prices by showing your
passport and either your return ticket or
departure card. For cigarettes and alcohol, your purchases will be sent to the
airport for you to collect when you leave
the country.

Ocean and beach safety

You'll find that the only real threat to your physical welfare in Barbados is the intense **Caribbean sun**. Many visitors get badly sunburned on the first day and suffer for the rest of their trip. To avoid this fate, it's advisable to wear a strong sunscreen at all times. Unprotected sun-worshippers should at least avoid the heat of the day between 11.30am and 2.30pm.

While you're on the beach, steer clear of the **manchineel trees**, recognizable by their shiny green leaves and the small, crab apple–like fruits that will be scattered around. The fruit is poisonous and, when it rains, the bark releases a sap that will cause blisters if it drips on you.

The sea, too, holds a handful of hazards. Don't worry about sharks or barracudas, which are rarely seen, but do watch out for **black sea urchins**, which are easily missed until you step on one in a patch of sea grass. If you walk on one and can't get the spines out, you'll need medical help.

Sport and leisure

Water sports fans are well provided for in Barbados – there are plenty of operators who offer excellent diving, snorkelling, waterskiing and similar activities. The island's windsurfing and surfing are also world-class, particularly on the southeast and east coasts, respectively. There are a number of land-based sports facilities on the island as well, including good golf courses, horse-riding stables, and excellent hiking trails.

For spectators, there is international cricket at the Kensington Oval (see p.64) between January and April each year, horseracing at the Garrison Savannah (see p.61) and a lively polo scene with matches at various venues including Holders House (see p.88). Look for the free annual *Sporting Barbados* magazine, available at the Barbados Tourism Authority in Bridgetown (see p.127) and at some hotels, which contains articles on the country's most popular sports.

Scuba-diving and snorkelling

Scuba-diving is excellent on the coral reefs around Barbados. The good sites are all off the calm west and south coasts, from Maycock's Bay in the north right round to Castle Bank near St Lawrence Gap; for descriptions of the main dive sites, visit Ⓦ www.divebarbados.net or Ⓦ www.diveprobarbados.com. The island has plenty of reputable dive operators, most of whom will lay on transport to and from your hotel. Prices can vary dramatically between diveshops – always cast around for the best deal – but reckon on around B$100 for a single-tank dive, B$180 for a two-tank dive and B$140 for a night dive, all including use of equipment.

Beginners can get a feel for diving by taking a half-day "**resort course**", involving basic theory, a shallow water (or pool) demonstration and a single dive. These courses cost around B$150, and allow you to continue to dive with the people who taught you, though not with any other operator.

Full **open-water certification** – involving theory, tests, training dives and four full dives – takes three to four days and usually costs around B$800. Serious divers may want to consider a package deal; some simply cover multiple dives (around B$500 for a six-dive package or B$850 for ten dives), while others include accommodation in addition to diving. Package prices can be pretty good value, with savings of up to twenty percent, particularly outside the winter season.

Snorkelling around Bardados is excellent, too, especially off the west coast, where there are plenty of good coralheads just offshore, notably at the Folkestone Marine Park (see p.92) and Paynes Bay (see p.86). If you want to go out to sea, find one of the several dive operators who take snorkellers on their dive trips – reckon on spending around B$30 for an outing, including equipment. Many top hotels provide guests with free snorkelling gear, but if you're not at one of these, buying the equipment can be expensive and you may just want to bring a mask and snorkel with you.

Scuba-diving companies

Dive Barbados Next to *Lone Star Restaurant* ☏422 3133, ✇www.divebarbados.net.
Divepro Barbados In *Oceans Restaurant*, St Lawrence Gap ☏420 3337, ✇www.diveprobarbados.com.
The Dive Shop Aquatic Gap, between *Hilton Barbados* and *Grand Barbados Beach Resort* ☏426 9947, ✇www.divebds.com.

Coral Reef Club ☏432 0931, ✇www.divehightide.com.

Boat trips

There is no shortage of **boat trips** to be made around Barbados, though the emphasis is normally on being part of a big crowd all having a fun time together – not, it must be said, everyone's cup of tea. The price normally includes a meal and/or "free" drinks, and entertainment – often including live music and shows – which usually kicks in at about the same time as the alcohol. The **catamarans** offer similar trips, though normally with a smaller number of people on board and less in the way of activities. All these boats sail out of Bridgetown's Shallow Harbour, just to the north of Deep Harbour, but most will pick up guests from any of the major resorts.

Boat companies

Cool Runnings Boats depart from Shallow Harbour ☏436 0911, ✇www.coolrunningsbarbados.com. This 45ft catamaran offers five-hour lunchtime snorkelling cruises (B$150), which take in the turtles in Paynes Bay and a shallow wreck just offshore, as well as four-hour sunset and snorkelling cruises along the coast (B$120). Food and drink are included in the price.
Harbour Master Boats depart from Shallow Harbour ☏430 0900, ✇www.tallshipscruises.com. Massive four-decker boat that runs a weekly day tour, taking you up the coast to a beach for chilling out or snorkelling, with a buffet lunch and free drinks (Wed 11am–4pm; B$130). It also runs an evening trip

---

Atlantis Submarine

It's rare that you have the opportunity to ride in a submarine, and rarer still that you can have an underwater adventure without getting wet, but the **Atlantis Submarine** allows you to do both. A boat takes you out of the Bridgetown Harbour to board the sub, which then submerges 30–45m, cruising slowly above the sea-bed for around forty minutes before rising to rejoin the "mother ship". Everyone has a seat by a port-hole, allowing for spectacular views of fish, coral and a shipwreck, and the co-pilot delivers a commentary on what you're seeing. Boats depart from Shallow Harbour. Tickets are B$170 per person and include pick-up from your hotel. For details and to make reservations, call ☏436 8929 or visit ✇www.atlantisadventures.com.

(Thurs 7–11pm; B$145), with a floor show, a live band, dinner and drinks all included in the price.

Jolly Roger Boats depart from Shallow Harbour ⓣ430 0900, ⓦwww.tallshipscruises.com. Sleek, two-sailed "pirate ship" that makes a weekly west coast lunch cruise (Sun 11am–3.30pm; B$115). The emphasis is on drinking, dancing, walking the plank and swinging from the yard-arm into the sea.

Silver Moon Boats depart from Shallow Harbour ⓣ438 2088, ⓦwww.oceanadventures.bb. Twelve- and eighteen-passenger capacities on the *Silver Moon* and the *Silver Moon II*, respectively, make these catamarans the pick of the west coast lunch cruises for those preferring an uncrowded, laid-back voyage. Snorkelling with turtles and plenty of food and drinks are included.

Tiami Boats depart from Shallow Harbour ⓣ430 0900, ⓦwww.tallshipscruises.com. Tiami has three catamarans that make daily west coast lunch cruises. The five-hour trip includes several beach/snorkelling stops as well as food and drink for B$150. A three-hour sunset cruise is also available every Sunday for $90.

Windsurfing and surfing

Barbados hosts regular **windsurfing** tournaments around Silver Sands on the south coast; the area is reckoned to be as good for windsurfers and kitesurfers as anywhere in the Caribbean. Many of the hotels here have their own windsurfers, which you can use – if you're staying there – at no extra cost. Alternatively, Charles Watersports in Dover (ⓣ428 9550) rents boards for B$25 per hour.

Surfing is also excellent, particularly on the east coast at the Bathsheba "soup bowl" (see p.120). Boards can be rented from a shack in Bathsheba called the *Soupbowl Café*, and you can occasionally buy them at the branch of the Cave Shepherd department store in the West Coast Mall in Holetown (ⓣ419 3110). The Barbados Surfing Association (ⓣ228 5117, ⓦwww.bsasurf.org) is a useful source of information, both for recreational surfers and for those wishing to compete in the competitions held on the island.

Fishing

Fishing is a way of life in Barbados, both as an industry and as a sport, so the island is an incomparable place to try your hand at it. Various charter boats offer deep-sea fishing trips on which you can go after wahoo, tuna, barracuda and, if you're lucky, marlin and other sailfish. The marlin season runs from the end of March to mid-June. Get an early start in the morning to maximize your chances of catching one. Prices for a group of up to six people start at around B$700 for a half-day, B$1200 for a whole day; rates include rods, bait, food, drink and transport from your hotel. If you are not part of a group, operators will fit you in with another party if they can, and charge around B$250–300 for a half-day. Regular operators include Billfisher II (ⓣ431 0741), Honey Bea III (ⓣ428 5344) and Blue Marlin Charters (ⓣ436 4322), but if you hunt around at dockside, particularly in Bridgetown, you can find plenty of others. Information on fishing tournaments held on the island is available from the Barbados Game Fishing Association (ⓦwww.barbadosgamefishing.com).

Other water sports

If you're after **waterskiing**, **jet-ski** rides or a speedy tow on an inflatable banana, most hotels can find a reputable operator for you – expect to pay around B$40 for a fifteen-minute banana-ride or B$100 for a half-hour of jet-skiing. Hightide Water-sports (ⓣ432 0931), at the *Coral Reef Club* on the west coast, is one of the most trustworthy operators. Another is Charles Watersports (ⓣ428 9550) at Dover Beach on the south coast. You'll also find guys with speedboats on many of the west coast beaches, though less so on the south coast where the water is often a bit too choppy. Bear in mind that though these operators are often cheaper, many of them are unlicensed and uninsured, and don't go with anyone unless you feel comfortable with their operation.

Similarly, you'll find locals offering trips on a **hobie-cat** (a mini-catamaran) on many of the beaches; they'll usually want to crew the boat themselves unless you can convince them you're an expert. Charles Watersports has one of the best selections of kit for rent, including kayaks for B$25 (single) or B$40 (double) per half-hour.

Finally, Falcon (☏ 419 0579, ⓦ www .parasailingwiththefalcon.com.bb) offers ten- to fifteen-minute **parasailing** trips – you're towed behind a boat on a parachute, then winched back aboard – from B$140 per person, or B$110 per person if you want to take someone up with you.

Hiking and biking

Some of the best and most scenic **hiking** in Barbados is along the beaches, particularly the east coast stretches between Martin's Bay and Bath (see p.117) and between Bathsheba (see p.119) and Cattlewash (see p.107). Free organized three-hour hikes are arranged by the Barbados National Trust, Wildey House, Wildey, St Michael (☏ 426 2421) every Sunday. There are three levels of hike – "Stop 'n Stare" (9.5km), "Here 'n There" (14.5km) and "Grin 'n Bear" (19.5km) – all starting at 6am, while at 3.30pm the "Stop 'n Stare" hike is repeated. On one Sunday per month, a moonlight hike leaves at 5.30pm (bring a torch). Routes vary each week, but often include places like Bottom Bay (see p.83), Turner's Hall Woods (see p.106) and Hackleton's Cliff (see p.118). This is an ideal way to see lesser known parts of the island and to meet Bajans, although note that to get to some of the departure points you'll need your own transport. A full programme of the year's hikes along with maps of the routes is available from the Barbados National Trust or at any branch of Butterfield Bank. The Barbados National Trust also organizes hikes along the excellent Arbib Nature and Heritage Trail around old Speightstown. If you

want to hike independently and off-the-beaten track, get hold of the 1:50,000 topographic map, available for B$15 from the Lands and Survey Department, Mahogany Court, Wildey Business Centre, Wildey (☏ 426 3959).

Bike tours are another good way of seeing the island. The Highland Adventure Centre organises enjoyable ninety-minute trips (☏ 438 8069) around Mount Hillaby and down to Cattlewash on the Atlantic coast; they cost B$90, are downhill all the way and include transport to and from your hotel.

Golf

There are two eighteen-hole **golf courses** open to the public in Barbados: one at Durants on the south coast and one on the west coast at Sandy Lane. It can be difficult to get a tee time at either course, particularly in high season, so it's worth planning ahead. The other major course, Royal Westmoreland, is only open to members and guests staying at certain of the more exclusive hotels. There is also a decent nine-hole course at Rockley on the south coast.

Golf courses

Barbados Golf Club Durants ☏ 428 8463, ⓦ www.barbadosgolfclub.com. Green fees are B$180, club rental a further B$50.

Club Rockley Barbados Rockley ☏ 435 7873, ⓦ www. rockleygolfclub.com. Green fees are B$76–96, club rental an additional B$24.

Sandy Lane Sandy Lane Bay ☏ 444 2222, Ⓕ 444 2000, ⓦ www.sandylane .com. Beautifully landscaped 6000m course. Green fees are B$350, club rental a further B$120.

Equestrian sports

Barbados has a lively equestrian tradition. There are usually one or two Saturday **races** per month at the Garrison Savannah racetrack (see p.61), and at Sandy Lane in March. The country has a few **polo** fields as well; the most prestigious of them, at Holders House (see p.88), holds matches from

September to March. For dates and times of matches, contact the Barbados Polo Club at ☎ 432 1802.

Not surprisingly, the island has several stables that give **riding tours**; most start around B$100. Good trips are organized by the Caribbean International Riding Centre, based in St Andrew parish (☎ 422 7433), which offers three options: an hour's tour of the Scotland District (B$100), a ninety-minute ride down to the beach (B$140) and a two-and-a-half-hour trip to the beach and back (B$180). Also worthwhile is the riding tour led by the Highland Adventure Centre (☎ 438 8069), located in St Thomas parish. The ninety-minute ride (B$120) travels past small villages and through sugar cane fields, in which green monkeys can often be spotted searching for food.

Clay pigeon and pistol shooting

Set on 70 acres just inland from the south coast in Carrington, a couple of kilometres west of Six Cross Roads, **Kendal Sporting** (☎ 437 5306, ⓦ www .go-kendal.com; Tues–Sun 10.30am–5pm) is a small members club that welcomes visitors for clay pigeon and pistol shooting. Coaching and safety advice are available to all, and the levels can be set from beginner to expert. Clay pigeon shooting costs B$85 for 25 rounds of ammunition and 25 clays; pistol shooting is B$60–90. There's a good restaurant and attractive pool as well, and non-shooters are welcome.

Cricket

If you're in Barbados for any length of time, you'll find it almost impossible to avoid the subject of **cricket**; more, perhaps, than anywhere else on earth, the game is *the* national passion. It was introduced to the island by the British military in the second half of the nineteenth century and today, alongside Jamaica and Trinidad, Barbados is one of the Big Three Caribbean cricketing nations. If you get the chance, catch a day of international cricket at the Kensington Oval in Bridgetown (see p.64). While the rest of the island slows to a near standstill, the otherwise stately stadium, completely revamped for its staging of the final of the 2007 Cricket World Cup, is transformed into a fairground, with music blaring, vendors hawking jerk chicken and Banks beer and a noisy crowd debating the finer points of the game. Listen out for the local cricketing lingo – a fielder placed out near the boundary, for example, is "in the country" – and for the lasting hoots of derision if anyone should spill a catch. The website of the West Indies Cricket Board, ⓦ www.windiescricket .com, has information on Caribbean cricket, including forthcoming matches and Barbados-specific cricketing news; for more opinionated articles, try ⓦ www .caribbeancricket.com.

The rules of cricket

Though the laws of cricket are complex, the basics are by no means as Byzantine as the game's detractors make out. The following are the bare rudiments of a sport whose beauty lies in the subtlety of its skills and tactics.

There are **two teams** of eleven players. A team wins by scoring more runs than the other team and dismissing all the opposition – in other words, a team could score many runs more than the opposition, but still not win if the last enemy batsman doggedly stays "in" (hence ensuring a draw). The match is divided into **innings**, when one team bats and the other fields. The number of innings varies depending on the type of competition: one-day matches have one per team, Test matches have two.

The aim of the fielding side is to limit the runs scored and get the batsmen "**out**". Two players from the batting side are on the pitch at any one time. The bowling side has a bowler, a wicketkeeper and nine fielders. Each inning is divided into overs, consisting of six deliveries, after which the wicketkeeper changes ends, the bowler is changed and the fielders move positions.

The batsmen **score runs** either by running up and down from wicket to wicket (one length = one run), or by hitting the ball over the boundary rope, scoring four runs if it crosses the boundary having touched the ground, and six runs if it flies over. The main ways a batsman can be dismissed are: by being "**clean bowled**", where the bowler dislodges the bails of the wicket

(the horizontal pieces of wood resting on top of the stumps); by being "**run out**", which is when one of the fielding side dislodges the bails with the ball while the batsman is running between the wickets; by being caught, which is when any of the fielding side catches the ball after the batsman has hit it and before it touches the ground; or "**lbw**" (leg before wicket), where the batsman blocks with his leg a delivery that would otherwise have hit his stumps.

Directory

Airport departure tax Departure tax is presently B$25, payable at the airport when you leave, in local currency only.
Banks Bridgetown: Butterfield Bank, Lower Broad St; Scotiabank, Broad St; Barbados National Bank, Broad St and Fairchild Street. Hastings: Scotiabank, opposite Skyway Plaza. Worthing: Scotiabank, beside the *Sandy Bay Beach Club*; Barbados National Bank, next to Club Xtreme. St Lawrence Gap: Royal Bank of Canada, by the *The Ship Inn* at the west end of the coast road. Holetown and Speightstown have numerous banks.
Electric current The island standard is 110 volts with two-pin sockets, though a few of the older hotels still use 220 volts. Take adaptors for essential items; some hotels have them, but you shouldn't count on it.
Emergencies Police ☎211; ambulance ☎511; fire brigade ☎311.
Hospitals Bridgetown has the six-hundred-bed public Queen Elizabeth Hospital (☎436 6450) and the private Bayview Hospital (☎436 5446), while smaller health centres and clinics are distributed

around the island; try the 24-hour-a-day Sandy Crest Medical Centre in Sunset Crest near Holetown (☎419 4911).
Laundry Bridgetown: Steve's, Bay St ☎427 9119 (Mon–Fri 8am–6pm, Sat 8am–3pm). Hastings: Hastings Village Laundromat, Balmoral Gap ☎429 7079 (Mon–Sat 8am–6pm, Sun 8am–2pm). Worthing: Worthing Laundromat, The Point View, just west of *Blue Horizons Hotel* ☎435 9501 (Mon-Fri 9am–5pm, Sat 9am–4.30pm). Speightstown: Tropical Laundries, opposite Jordan's Plaza ☎422 2489 (Mon–Fri 8am–1pm & 2–5pm, Sat 8am–1pm & 2–4pm).
Newspapers The two daily papers, the *Advocate* (◍www.barbadosadvocate.com) and the *Nation* (◍www.nationnews.com), concentrate on domestic news, though there is a token gesture towards international news coverage and, invariably, a big sports section.
Pharmacies Bridgetown: Knight's, Lower Broad St ☎426 5196 (Mon–Sat 8am–5pm). Holetown: Knight's, inside the supermarket at West Coast Mall ☎432 1290 (Mon–Sat 8am–7pm, Sun 9am–1pm). Oistins: Knight's, Southern

Fly Less – Stay Longer!

Rough Guides believes in the good that travel does, but we are deeply aware of the impact of fuel emissions on climate change. We recommend taking fewer trips and staying for longer. If you can avoid travelling by air, please use an alternative, especially for journeys of under 1000km/600miles. And always offset your travel at ◍www.roughguides.com/climatechange.

Plaza ☎428 6057 (Mon–Sat 8am–8pm). Rockley: Lewis' Drug Mart, opposite the *Accra Beach Hotel* ☎435 8090 (Mon–Fri 9am–6pm, Sat 9am–1pm, Sun 9am–noon). Speightstown: Knight's (☎422 0048 Mon–Thurs & Sun 8am–5pm, Fri 8am–7pm).

Radio Radio stations include the public service channel Voice of Barbados (92.9 FM), and the BBS (90.7 FM), both of which carry news, sport, chat shows and music, mostly international hits with a sprinkling of Bajan tunes. The most entertaining show is Voice of Barbados's lively and outspoken phone-in *Down to Brass Tacks*, which goes out every day at 11.30am.

Time Barbados is on the Atlantic time zone, four hours behind Greenwich Mean Time in winter (Oct-Apr) and five hours behind GMT in summer (May-Sept).

Tipping and taxes Many hotels and restaurants automatically add a service charge of ten percent, so check your bill to ensure you're not paying twice. At restaurants that don't do this, tipping is not usually expected but (of course) always appreciated. All prices, whether in restaurants or shops, include fifteen percent government tax.

TV The local station is shown on channel 8, while many hotels and sports bars carry satellite TV (mostly programmes from North America).

Travel store

Available from all good bookstores D: Rough Guide DIRECTIONS

For more information go to www.roughguides.com

www.roughguides.com

Information on over 25,000 destinations around the world

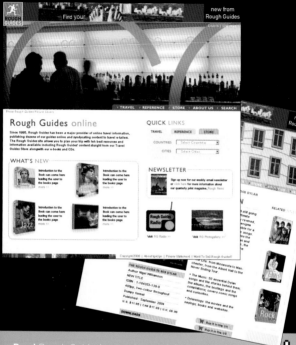

- **Read** Rough Guides' trusted travel info

- **Access** exclusive articles from Rough Guides authors

- **Update** yourself on new books, maps, CDs and other products

- **Enter** our competitions and win travel prizes

- **Share** ideas, journals, photos & travel advice with other users

- **Earn** points every time you contribute to the Rough Guide
  community and get rewards

Listen Up!

"You may be used to the Rough Guide series being comprehensive, but nothing will prepare you for the exhaustive Rough Guide to World Music . . . one of our books of the year."

Sunday Times, London

Rough Guide Music Titles

The Beatles • Blues • Bob Dylan • Classical Music
Elvis • Frank Sinatra • Heavy Metal • Hip-Hop
iTunes, iTunes & music online • Jazz
Book of Playlists • Opera • Pink Floyd • Punk
Reggae • Rock • The Rolling Stones
Soul and R&B • World Music Vol 1 & 2

small print & Index

A Rough Guide to Rough Guides

In 1981, Mark Ellingham, a recent graduate in English from Bristol University, was travelling in Greece on a tiny budget and couldn't find the right guidebook. With a group of friends he wrote his own guide, combining a contemporary, journalistic style with a practical approach to travellers' needs. That first Rough Guide was a student scheme that became a publishing phenomenon. Today, Rough Guides include recommendations from shoestring to luxury and cover hundreds of destinations around the globe, including almost every country in the Americas and Europe, more than half of Africa and most of Asia and Australasia. Millions of readers relish Rough Guides' wit and inquisitiveness as much as their enthusiastic, critical approach and value-for-money ethos. The guides' ever-growing team of authors and photographers is spread all over the world.

In the early 1990s, Rough Guides branched out of travel, with the publication of Rough Guides to World Music, Classical Music and the Internet. All three have become benchmark titles in their fields, spearheading the publication of a range of more than 350 titles under the Rough Guide name, including phrasebooks, waterproof maps, music guides from Opera to Heavy Metal, reference works as diverse as Conspiracy Theories and Shakespeare, and popular culture books from iPods to Poker. Rough Guides also produce a series of more than 120 World Music CDs in partnership with World Music Network.

Visit www.roughguides.com to see our latest publications.

Rough Guide travel images are available for commercial licensing at www.roughguidespictures.com

Publishing information

This second edition published April 2007 by Rough Guides Ltd, 80 Strand, London WC2R 0RL. 345 Hudson St, 4th Floor, New York, NY 10014, USA.

Distributed by the Penguin Group
Penguin Books Ltd, 80 Strand, London WC2R 0RL
Penguin Group (USA), 375 Hudson Street, NY 10014, USA
14 Local Shopping Centre, Panchsheel Park, New Delhi 110017, India
Penguin Group (Australia), 250 Camberwell Road, Camberwell, Victoria 3124, Australia
Penguin Group (Canada), 10 Alcorn Avenue, Toronto, ON M4V 1E4, Canada
Penguin Group (NZ), 67 Apollo Drive, Mairangi Bay, Auckland 1310, New Zealand
Typeset in Bembo and Helvetica to an original design by Henry Iles.
Cover concept by Peter Dyer.
Printed and bound in China

160pp includes index

A catalogue record for this book is available from the British Library

ISBN 13: 978-1-84353-774-8

The publishers and authors have done their best to ensure the accuracy and currency of all the information in Barbados DIRECTIONS, however, they can accept no responsibility for any loss, injury, or inconvenience sustained by any traveller as a result of information or advice contained in the guide.

3   5   7   9   8   6   4   2

Help us update

We've gone to a lot of effort to ensure that the second edition of Barbados DIRECTIONS is accurate and up-to-date. However, things change – places get "discovered", opening hours are notoriously fickle, restaurants and rooms raise prices or lower standards. If you feel we've got it wrong or left something out, we'd like to know, and if you can remember the address, the price, the phone number, so much the better.
We'll credit all contributions, and send a copy of the next edition (or any other DIRECTIONS guide or Rough Guide if you prefer) for the best letters. Everyone who writes to us and isn't already a subscriber will receive a copy of our full-colour thrice-yearly newsletter. Please mark letters: "Barbados DIRECTIONS Update" and send to: Rough Guides, 80 Strand, London WC2R 0RL, or Rough Guides, 345 Hudson St, New York, NY 10014. Or send an email to mail@ roughguides.com
Have your questions answered and tell others about your trip at www.roughguides.atinfopop.com

Rough Guide credits

Text editor: Ella Steim
Layout: Pradeep Thapliyal
Photography: Martin Richardson, Ian Cumming
Cartography: Amod Singh, Katie Lloyd-Jones
Picture editor: Harriet Mills

Proofreader: Anita Sach
Production: Aimee Hampson
Design: Henry Iles
Cover design: Chloë Roberts

SMALL PRINT

The author

Adam Vaitilingam is the author of many books on the Caribbean. He lives in Bristol.

Acknowledgements

Ross Velton would like to thank Hamish Watson, Brigitte Taylor, and Renée Coppin, as well as Dr Nigel Roberts, Godfrey Reid, Doris Nurse, and Ocean Adventures. The conscientious editing of Ella Steim is also appreciated.

Index

Maps are marked in colour